At Issue

Are Natural Disasters Increasing?

Other Books in the At Issue Series:

At Issue

Are Natural Disasters Increasing?

Stefan Kiesbye, Book Editor

GREENHAVEN PRESS
A part of Gale, Cengage Learning

Detroit • New York • San Francisco • New Haven, Conn • Waterville, Maine • London

Christine Nasso, *Publisher*
Elizabeth Des Chenes, *Managing Editor*

For more information, contact:
Greenhaven Press
27500 Drake Rd.
Farmington Hills, MI 48331-3535
Or you can visit our Internet site at gale.cengage.com

For product information and technology assistance, contact us at

Gale Customer Support, 1-800-877-4253
For permission to use material from this text or product, submit all requests online at www.cengage.com/permissions

Further permissions questions can be emailed to permissionrequest@cengage.com

Articles in Greenhaven Press anthologies are often edited for length to meet page requirements. In addition, original titles of these works are changed to clearly present the main thesis and to explicitly indicate the author's opinion. Every effort is made to ensure that Greenhaven Press accurately reflects the original intent of the authors. Every effort has been made to trace the owners of copyrighted material.

Cover image © Sue Poynton. Image from BigStockPhoto.com.

LIBRARY OF CONGRESS CATALOGING-IN-PUBLICATION DATA

Are natural disasters increasing? / Stefan Kiesbye, book editor.
   p. cm. -- (At issue)
  Includes bibliographical references and index.
  ISBN 978-0-7377-4665-5 (hardcover) -- ISBN 978-0-7377-4666-2 (pbk.)
  1. 1. Natural disasters--Juvenile literature. I. I. Kiesbye, Stefan.
  GB5019.A74 2010
  363.34--dc22

                                     2009042506

Printed in the United States of America
1 2 3 4 5 6 7 14 13 12 11 10

Contents

Introduction

In November of 2008, several wildfires sprang up in Southern California, from Orange County to Santa Barbara. Hundreds of homes burned down, and for days, people could smell and see the smoke of the surrounding blazes, even in downtown Los Angeles. Tens of thousands of people were evacuated, many weren't able to return home for days and weeks. Others returned to smoldering ruins. The fire in Sylmar, known as the Sayre Fire, destroyed the Oakridge Mobile Home Park, often called the Beverly Hills of mobile homes for its beauty and serenity. The *Los Angeles Times* wrote that, "Oakridge was a broad panorama of ash and twisted metal. Broken water lines gushed and sprayed like artesian wells. When Fernando Corral, 44, decided to return to his family's mobile home community, he knew exactly where to go. Standing about 200 yards from the main entrance and leaning against a small chain-link fence, Corral, his wife, and son Jonathan, 13, looked directly at their destroyed home. 'Pretty, isn't it?' he asked as he turned his head away from the blowing ash. A few feet away lay a charred piano songbook, 'Beautiful Dreamer.' 'I never liked that song,' Jonathan Corral said. 'It was too hard.'"

About 10,000 people were evacuated, and many watched on television how their homes were devoured by flames. More than 500 mobile homes were burnt.

In September of that same year, Hurricane Ike had devastated parts of Cuba and made landfall in Galveston, Texas. *ABC News* reported on September 15 that, "Ike's 100 mph winds and 16 inches of rain hit the Texas coast Saturday morning (Sept. 13). The storm's surge—a nearly 13-foot wall of water—was much lower than had been predicted but still more than enough to put most of Galveston underwater, obliterate thousands of homes, and rain sheets of glass shards down on the streets of Houston, the nation's fourth largest city. Most of Houston remains without power today. Authorities estimate that 140,000 people ignored mandatory evacuation orders; despite having to deal with flooded streets and houses, officials have rescued 2,000 people and several stranded pets so far. The air space from Houston to Galveston was closed for most of the day Sunday, allowing air traffic for rescue operations only."

Natural catastrophes are not made—they happen. And yet they seem to be more frequent and more deadly. Climate change—caused by carbon emissions and other factors—might play into the more recent disasters, but people might be influencing the devastating effects of them more directly—simply by living in areas known to be targets of storms and fires.

The topic has many facets, and is engulfed in class, race, and political issues. For example, in New Orleans, the areas hit worst by Hurricane Katrina in 2005 were populated by the city's poor, often black, citizens. And the lack of quick, federal help broke open old wounds and had many people asking if the George W. Bush administration's slow response showed signs of racism.

The homes destroyed by California wildfires are often expensive ones, built by people who have the money to move away from cities and suburbs. But no matter where one looks—to homes in Iowa swept away by floods, or to the coasts of Thailand, India and Sri Lanka, which were hit by the 2004 tsunami—there are people living in potentially dangerous areas, with often inefficient warning systems and even worse evacuation plans, if any exist at all. Driven by poverty, or enabled by affluence, people build homes where no safe living is possible.

While disaster planning and disaster response can be much improved, many people might face the prospect of climagration—the evacuation and relocation of entire communities because of climate change or natural disasters. The British

Guardian writes that, "in 2006, the US government completed a $2.5m seawall to protect the [Alaskan] native village of Kivalina, located on an island in the Chukchi Sea. But on the day of the dedication ceremony, a storm surge partly destroyed the newly constructed sea barrier. One year later, the community was evacuated to protect inhabitants from a severe storm ... Approximately 200 indigenous villages that have inhabited the arctic for millennia are located along Alaska's coasts and rivers. Dozens of these communities are now endangered because of accelerating erosion and flooding. Five indigenous communities, located along the Bering and Chukchi Seas, have concluded that relocation is the only durable solution to the climatic events that are threatening their lives." Global warming might displace these villages, but the effects of climate change can be felt elsewhere too. According to the *Guardian*, "Catastrophic random environmental events, such as hurricanes, do not cause climigration. However, these random environmental events, if on-going, may alter ecosystems permanently, cause extensive damage to public infrastructure, repeatedly place people in danger and require communities to relocate. Determining which communities are most likely to encounter displacement will require a complex assessment of a community's ecosystem vulnerability to climate change, as well as the vulnerability of its social, economic and political structures. Permanent relocation must only occur when there are no other durable solutions."

In *At Issue: Are Natural Disasters Increasing?*, the authors of the following viewpoints debate a variety of issues on this pressing topic.

1

Natural Disasters Are Increasing in Quantity and Severity

Environment Canada

Environment Canada's mandate is to preserve and enhance the quality of the natural environment; conserve Canada's renewable resources; conserve and protect Canada's water resources; forecast weather and environmental change; enforce rules relating to boundary waters; and coordinate environmental policies and programs for the federal government.

Weather-related disasters have increased dramatically in Canada, and population growth and urbanization have contributed to their devastating effects. Ironically, technological advances have led people to build homes in hazard-prone areas, thus adding to the disasters' impacts. Education is more important than technology to decrease the population's vulnerability to natural disasters. Furthermore, some communities should be relocated to avoid future risks.

In 2002, natural disasters caused approximately $85 billion in economic losses worldwide—up 36 per cent over the previous year. Last summer [2002], parts of Europe experienced the worst floods in centuries, while Western Canada struggled through the most devastating drought in its recorded history.

Last year, the world experienced approximately 700 natural disasters—50 more than the annual average during the 1990s.

Environment Canada, "Natural Disasters on the Rise," *The Science and the Environment Bulletin*, March/April 2003. Reproduced by permission.

The magnitude of the events that occurred and recent trends lend weight to the fact that such incidents are growing not only in number, but also in size.

Over the past decade, Canada has experienced many of its largest natural disasters, and experts believe that even bigger and more devastating ones are inevitable. While geophysical disasters, such as earthquakes, have remained relatively constant in this country over the past 50 years, weather-related disasters have skyrocketed. Climate change is projected to exacerbate this situation in future, as it is expected to increase the frequency and severity of some extreme weather events.

Researching Disasters

To examine this trend and help determine ways to mitigate its risks, a team of public- and private-sector partners, led by Environment Canada's Meteorological Service of Canada, formed the Canadian Natural Hazards Assessment Project. Key players include the Office of Critical Infrastructure Protection and Emergency Preparedness, the Institute for Catastrophic Loss Reduction, private insurance companies, emergency responders, academics, sociologists, and engineers.

After more than three years of collecting and analyzing data, the project team has written 20 technical papers on the subject, most of which will be published early this year [2003] in a special edition of the *Journal of Natural Hazards*. Also scheduled for release by this spring is a summary document for decision makers and members of the public.

Higher concentrations of people living in urban areas means that if disasters do hit, they affect a larger number of individuals.

The team's findings indicate that a combination of factors are behind this upward trend, not only in Canada, but also around the world. Chief among these is the fact that human beings have greatly increased their vulnerability to suffering some degree of loss from a hazardous event. This has occurred due to the many economic, socio-demographic, and technological changes that have taken place over the past 50 years.

For example, by exploiting our natural resources, humans have degraded the environment and destroyed natural buffers that help to reduce the impacts of certain hazards. Greenhouse-gas emissions from the burning of fossil fuels are changing our climate. The cutting of timber on hillsides is magnifying the impact of landslides. The draining of wetlands has amplified the effects of flooding.

Ever-Increasing Vulnerability

Population growth and urbanization are also major contributors to our increase in vulnerability. Higher concentrations of people living in urban areas means that if disasters do hit, they affect a larger number of individuals. Urban sprawl has led to more development in high-risk areas, such as flood plains. Over-reliance on technologies, such as structures that divert floodwaters, has also encouraged development that might otherwise not have taken place—making the potential impact of a disaster even greater. Other factors include our aging population and our aging infrastructure, both of which are more susceptible to harm.

Data show that just over half of all Canadian disasters—whether natural or not—have been weather related, and that this percentage has increased drastically in recent years. Virtually all of the most expensive natural disasters this country has experienced fall into this weather-related category.

As in the rest of the world, floods are the main cause of the increase in the number of natural disasters in Canada, despite the fact that their impacts are largely avoidable. Snow-melt accounts for about 40 per cent of all floods in Canada, although they can also be caused or compounded by heavy rainfall, ice jams, glacier outbursts, coastal storms, tsunamis, cyclones, and hurricanes.

Drought is Canada's most expensive natural disaster in a cumulative sense.

While some research suggests that a greater percentage of Canada's rainfall is occurring in heavy downpours, much responsibility for the upward trend in flood disasters is our own. Flooding in urban areas has been greatly exacerbated by extensive paving (which reduces the penetration of water into the ground), aging sewer systems that are less able to cope with larger loads, and the construction of roads, homes, and other structures on flood plains.

Improvements in Planning Are Needed

Forecasts can be useful in lessening the impact of flood events, but improved flood-plain mapping, land-use planning, and the use of structural defenses are even more effective. For example, the Red River Floodway, which was constructed in the 1960s to protect Winnipeg from flooding, has been used more than 20 times since—and saved an estimated $6 billion during the Red River Flood of 1997.

Drought is Canada's most expensive natural disaster in a cumulative sense. Over 40 severe events have occurred over the past 200 years in Western Canada alone, and a number have taken place in other parts of the country as well. Four of the six most expensive natural disasters in Canada's history were droughts—and all four took place within the last 25 years.

Droughts can be related to reduced streamflow, water levels, runoff, or soil moisture, but most are caused by disruptions in normal weather patterns that result in below-normal precipitation. They can be self-perpetuating, since areas experiencing drought add little water vapour to the local atmosphere. Droughts can't be predicted, but their impacts can be lessened through such efforts as water and soil conservation, grassland management, and forest-fire watches.

Although the only significant earthquake in Canada occurred off the East Coast in 1929, triggering a tsunami that killed 28 people, scientists predict that an earthquake in the Vancouver area is the most likely major disaster on our horizon. Since quakes occur where tectonic plates converge, only certain regions of the country are at risk: the West Coast, the St. Lawrence and Ottawa valleys, off the coast of Nova Scotia and Newfoundland, and certain parts of the Arctic.

Quakes are also unpredictable, but maps of their probability can be created using databases of past locations and magnitudes, and geotechnical models. These maps allow for the design of appropriate building codes, as well as the avoidance of development in potentially hazardous areas.

The findings of the Canadian Natural Hazards Assessment Project clearly indicate that mitigating the risks of natural disasters in Canada requires more than advancements in science and technology. It requires us to create a culture that is aware of disasters and their risks, and that considers them at all levels of decision making. It requires the implementation of non-structural steps, such as the preservation of the natural environment, public education, and the relocation of communities to areas that are not hazard-prone.

Most importantly, we must address the large gaps that exist in our understanding of the vulnerability of different regions of Canada by creating an interdisciplinary hazards community that involves both the physical and social sciences. By being aware of natural hazards and how the decisions we make affect our vulnerability, the human and economic toll they impose upon us can be greatly reduced.

2

Natural Disasters Are On the Rise

Theresa Braine

Theresa Braine is a journalist who covers global health and other topics.

Disasters have increased, due to routine and man-made climate change, and are heavily influenced by socioeconomic factors. Since the world population has increased steadily, more and more people, and especially the poor, are effected by natural disasters. While disasters have always been part of the human experience, climate change clearly influences the frequency of droughts and storms. Countries need to step up their disaster preparedness and education if future disasters are to be avoided.

Tsunamis, hurricanes and typhoons, earthquakes, locusts and now the threat of a flu pandemic—will 2005 be remembered as the year of natural disasters?

The year 2005 saw the aftermath of the 26 December 2004 earthquake and tsunami waves in Asia, hurricanes in Central and North America, notably Katrina, which triggered flooding in the US city of New Orleans, and the 8 October earthquake in Pakistan and India. The year also saw famine after crops were destroyed by locusts in Niger.

Virtually unnoticed by the outside world was tiny El Salvador where the country's highest volcano, Ilamatepec, erupted on 1 October, displacing more than 7,500 people and killing

Theresa Braine, "Was 2005 the Year of Natural Disasters?" *The Panama News*, vol. 12, January 8–21, 2006. Copyright © 2006 by Eric Jackson. Originally published by the World Health Organization. Reproduced by permission.

two. A few days later Hurricane Stan swept through and killed about 70 people with floods and mudslides.

From January to October 2005, an estimated 97,490 people were killed in disasters globally and 88,117 of them in natural disasters, according to the Center for Research on the Epidemiology of Disasters (CRED), a WHO [World Health Organization] Collaborating Centre that operates a global disaster database in Belgium. According to CRED, the number of natural disasters—floods, windstorms, droughts and geological disasters—recorded since 1900 have increased and the number of people affected by such disasters has also increased since 1975.

Some disasters experts reject the term "natural disasters," arguing that there is almost always a man-made element.

Disasters Appear to Happen More Frequently

Is this as bad as it gets, or could it get worse? Why do natural disasters appear to be increasingly frequent and increasingly deadly?

Today's disasters stem from a complex mix of factors, including routine climate change, global warming influenced by human behavior, socioeconomic factors causing poorer people to live in risky areas, and inadequate disaster preparedness and education on the part of governments as well as the general population.

Some disasters experts reject the term "natural disasters," arguing that there is almost always a man-made element.

"I don't like to use the term 'natural disasters,'" said Dr. Ciro Ugarte, Regional Advisor for Emergency Preparedness and Disaster Relief with the Pan American Health Organization (PAHO) in Washington, DC, explaining that natural disasters would not have such a devastating effect on people's lives if they were not exposed to such risks in the first place.

Natural phenomena do not always generate human disasters. Ugarte noted that in 2005, several earthquakes that struck in South America were of a higher magnitude than the one that devastated northern Pakistan and parts of India in October, but these hit sparsely populated areas and therefore caused less damage. The same goes for several tsunamis in 2005 which were not deemed "disasters" because they didn't endanger anyone, Ugarte said.

Overpopulation Increases Vulnerability

Natural phenomena are likely to affect more people because Earth's population has increased. According to the United Nations Population Fund, this stands at about 6.5 billion people and is projected to reach 9.1 billion people in 2050.

Marko Kokic, spokesperson for WHO's Health Action in Crisis department, said that some communities are more vulnerable to the effects of natural disasters than 100 years ago because of ecological degradation. He said that, for example, when tropical storms hit the Caribbean in September 2004, there was nothing to stop storm waters gathering and wreaking devastation in Haiti because of deforestation.

"We need to tackle the underlying issues, such as poverty and inequity," Kokic said, adding: "In many countries, people cut down trees because wood is the cheapest fuel."

Disasters are also a consequence of development and industrialization. In Europe, experts believe that countries such as France and Germany are more adversely affected by floods today because major rivers, such as the Rhine, have been straightened to ease commercial traffic.

Global warming as well as routine, cyclical climate changes are causing a higher number of strong hurricanes in the Caribbean, meteorologists say. Add to that the increasing number of people living in areas such as coastlines, in substandard housing and the destruction in a crisis of essential infrastructure, such as hospitals, and you have the potential for more devastating disasters than a few decades ago.

There have always been disasters. The bubonic plague wiped out more than 25 million people or 37 percent of Europe's population, in the 1300s. More recently, the 1918–19 flu pandemic killed between 20 and 40 million people worldwide. One of the earliest recorded disasters, the eruption of Vesuvius in 79 AD, buried the ancient Roman city of Pompeii killing about 10,000 people. Today, two million people live within its possible range, illustrating one major difference between then and now.

Some experts believe the most practical approach to preparedness may be to focus on reducing the risks rather than factors behind the risks.

Risk Reduction Might Prove Most Effective

About 75 disasters were reported globally in 1975, according to CRED. In 2000 the figure peaked at 525 and dropped to just under 400 in 2004. By far the highest number of fatalities—about 450,000—occurred in 1984. In 2004 nearly 300,000 died in disasters, but the number of people affected has soared since 1975 with about 600 million people affected by disasters of all kinds in 2002.

So complex and intertwined are the factors behind these disasters that some experts believe the most practical approach to preparedness may be to focus on reducing the risks rather than factors behind the risks.

Dave Paul Zervaas, regional coordinator for Latin America and the Caribbean at the United Nations' International Strategy for Disaster Reduction (ISDR), argued that preparation should focus on making people less vulnerable to disasters.

"We think it's much more important now to look at vulnerabilities, because you have factors you can control," Zervaas said. "You can work to lower vulnerability [to disasters]."

Hurricane Katrina in the United States is a good example, Zervaas said. A number of factors contributed to the damage and loss of life. The storm was huge. It struck a city whose levees had not been maintained or strengthened for years, and government agencies' response to the emergency was at first inadequate.

In Central America storms such as hurricanes Mitch and Stan have wrought damage with rain and landslides rather than wind. "The poverty issue and the social inequity situation have not become much better in most places," said Zervaas, adding that migration to cities conspires with a lack of urban planning to put people in danger.

Climate Change Affects Disasters

Clearly, climate change—whether helped by human behavior or not—is playing a role. Hurricane experts say the world is in the midst of a routine, cyclical climate change that causes the Caribbean to heat up, increasing the frequency of powerful storms. The effect of this is greater than that of global warming, according to Stanley Goldenberg, a meteorologist at the US National Oceanic and Atmospheric Administration in Miami.

While earthquakes represent some of the most devastating disasters in recent years, these are diminishing in strength compared with earlier times, Ugarte said. Nowadays an earthquake with a magnitude of 8, 9 or 10 on the Richter scale is rare, the one in south Asia in October 2005 was 7.6, Ugarte said, adding: "But yes, we are seeing a lot of damage. You will probably find more damage in the future for phenomena that are less in magnitude than in previous years."

Experts agree that the poor are disproportionately hit. "In several of these countries, the poor people are looking for spaces to build their houses or their communities [and] they find spaces that are not already used," Ugarte said. "And those spaces that are not already used are usually the spaces at higher risk for natural phenomena. There's a huge relationship between this kind of damage and poverty."

For this reason financial services play a role in both prevention, and damage limitation and recovery. A report entitled, *Climate Change Futures: Health Ecological and Economic Dimensions*, published in November 2005 assesses the risks generated by climate change. One of several scenarios "would involve blows to the world economy sufficiently severe to cripple the resilience that enables affluent countries to respond to catastrophes," according to the report, which was published by the Center for Health and Global Environment at the Harvard Medical School and sponsored by reinsurance company Swiss Re and the United Nations Development Program. While it is important to encourage people, governments and companies to buy insurance, not everyone can afford it or see the need.

Microfinancing is another avenue, giving poor people the means to improve their economic situation so that a disaster does not hit them as hard as it would otherwise, and also by lending them money to use in recovering from it.

Improving Disaster Preparedness

Many countries are working to improve their disaster preparedness, but more needs to be done, Ugarte said.

"Countries are now better prepared in comparison to 1970," he said. "But now the level of preparation and risk reduction that you need is huge in comparison to that year."

The Michoacan earthquake in Mexico in 1985 showed that being well prepared was not enough because hospitals in the disaster zone were destroyed. Likewise, in Grenada Hurricane Ivan damaged and disrupted much of the Caribbean island's health system, making it difficult for health workers to respond to the needs generated by the hurricane.

Early warning systems and education are essential to prevent and mitigate against the effects of natural disasters.

PAHO has expanded its programs to focus not only on preparedness but also on mitigation. This involves reducing secondary deaths and destruction that can occur in the aftermath of a disaster, and implementing building codes that require hospitals, schools, military bases [and] other vital structures to be built to withstand such disasters.

Many countries say they can't afford more preparation, but some measures are simple and can be inexpensive, such as a tsunami warning system, Ugarte said. "But from there to Banda Aceh, that is another step," Ugarte said, referring to the capital of the Indonesian province that was worst hit by the earthquake and tsunami of December 2004. "And from Banda Aceh to all the little communities on the coast, that's another issue. That last link of the chain is not in place. And that is the system that we need to build."

Disaster experts say early warning systems and education are essential to prevent and mitigate against the effects of natural disasters. In its World Disasters Report 2005, the International Federation of Red Cross and Red Crescent Societies notes that a simple phone call saved thousands of lives when the giant tsunami waves hit India in 2004. A fisherman's son named Vijayakumar Gunasekaran, who lives in Singapore, heard about the tsunami early on the radio and phoned relatives living on the east coast of India. Following his warning, all 3,630 residents evacuated their village there before the waves arrived.

3

Natural Disasters Have Always Been a Problem

Patrick J. Michaels

Patrick J. Michaels is a senior fellow in environmental studies at the Cato Institute and author of Meltdown: The Predictable Distortion of Global Warming by Scientists, Politicians, and the Media.

Natural disasters have been recorded throughout the ages— sometimes perceived as necessary regulators of forests—and climate change is the media's newfound culprit. Despite evidence to the contrary, scientists today prefer to blame man-made climate change instead of naturally occurring changes. Civilization has changed the make-up of our ecology and how it is affected by disasters, yet it has not changed the frequency of hurricanes or the global temperature.

Hurricane Katrina—a very big storm by any measure—has now been called the "largest ecological disaster in U.S. history," according to the *Christian Science Monitor*, because it "killed or damaged about 320 million trees." Moreover, Katrina was a double ecological whammy, as the downed trees will eventually rot or burn, releasing another increment (probably too small to detect) of dreaded carbon dioxide, the main global warming gas. The *Monitor*'s report was based upon an analysis of satellite imagery conducted by scientists at the University of New Hampshire.

Patrick J. Michaels, "Unnatural History," *American Spectator*, November 28, 2008. Reproduced by permission.

Wait a minute. Hurricanes have been a fact of life for the forests of southeastern North America ever since there were forests, and that's a pretty long time.

Disasters Are Natural

The natural vegetation of the coastal southeast consists largely of a mixture of Pine and Oak species. That's not what it is today, because today's vegetation isn't natural. Rather, it's virtually all a commercial mix of softwoods designed to grow fast and tall, so the trees can quickly be sawed into houses. Today's forest probably maintains a higher vertical profile than the one that was here before, and it's also largely protected from fire, but not from hurricanes.

Back before us, believe it or not, weather was pretty much the same as it is now.

Back before us, believe it or not, weather was pretty much the same as it is now. Consider the very severe drought currently plaguing the Deep South. Remember those forest fires in Georgia late last summer? The only reason they didn't burn down most of the state's forests was that they were unnaturally extinguished.

It's fair to say that the integrated intensity of the southeastern drought may be a one-in-fifty year occurrence. That would mean, in a "natural" world (i.e., one without human sprawl) a southeastern forest would go about fifty years before combusting.

Or, perhaps, taken down by a hurricane. Pines and oaks have been around about 100 million years. Hurricanes have been around longer.

Here's the cool part: the present era. Ninety-five percent of the last 100 million years were warmer than now. It's only about 5 million years or so ago that we began to slip into the current ice-age climate (from which carbon dioxide may mercifully extricate us, some say).

Now, just for fun, let's assume that Katrina was a product of global warming. Forget that no scientist will stand up and point the causative finger. But, if it was, Katrina was therefore typical of many hurricanes of the last 100 million years. In other words, the natural southern forest evolved in a world studded with Katrinas.

Not Every Disaster Is an Ecological Catastrophe

Part of the modern climate mythology is the assumption that every significant climate burp, such as the big El Niño of 1998, or the big hurricane season of 2005 is portentous of ecological disaster. Hardly. In fact, if today's species were not adapted to these extremes, they simply wouldn't be here.

It's almost too bad that we don't have the "natural" forest of southeastern North America anymore. I'll bet, if we did, that some ecological researcher would have discovered indeed that such a forest in fact *requires* hurricanes, just as the flowering plants of the desert southwest *require* El Niño rains for germination and subsequent reproduction.

Weather and climate are now assumed to be driving the world into ecological chaos.

There once was a concept of "potential natural vegetation" of the United States, which was thought to be what would eventually appear in the absence of human management. The modern view of forest dynamics is somewhat different, but, nonetheless, the "natural" distribution of the oak-pine forest pretty much corresponds to the inland reach of the strongest hurricanes.

OK, that was my original Ph.D. topic proposal, back in a 1971 paper at the University of Chicago. It was laughed at, because, at the time, ecologists didn't think weather or climate were very important modulators of ecosystem behavior. Four years later, the surface temperature of the planet began to rise. About a third of a century later, a hurricane was blamed for the largest ecological disaster in our history.

Now it's the other way around. Weather and climate are now assumed to be driving the world into ecological chaos. It seems reasonable that, say, 30 years from now, something else will be to blame.

Finally, whenever a hurricane (or a fire) takes down a forest, it's not replaced by anything but another forest. That vegetation will absorb some of the carbon dioxide that Katrina's trees left behind. It will eventually look a lot like the one that got blown down, only to await the sawmill, or the next big hurricane.

4

Climate Change Will Lead to Many Disasters

John Vidal

John Vidal is the Guardian's *environment editor. He is the author of* McLibel: Burger Culture on Trial *and has contributed chapters to books on topics such as the Gulf war, new Europe and development.*

While many developed nations profit from climate change, poor countries suffer from extended droughts and other weather-related disasters. Small-scale farmers are ruined, while others are threatened by severe hurricanes or cyclones. Food production is decreasing, which further aggravates the situation. If the developed nations don't offer help, countries like Bangladesh or Brazil might soon face emergency situations.

Joao da Antonio's eyes are full of tears. If good rains do not come, he says, he will pack his bag, kiss his wife and two children goodbye and join the annual exodus of young men leaving hot, dry rural north-east Brazil for the biofuel fields in the south.

Da Antonio, 19, can earn about £30 a month for 10 hours gruelling work a day cutting sugar cane to make ethanol, and more than a million small farmers like him migrate south for six months of the year because the land can no longer support them. Tens of thousands a year never return, forced to move permanently to Sao Paulo or another of Brazil's cities in search of work.

John Vidal, "Wetter and Wilder: The Signs of Warning Everywhere," *The Guardian*, December 10, 2008. Reproduced by permission of Guardian News Service, LTD.

"Life here is one of suffering," Da Antonio said. "I will do anything to earn some money. None of us want to die, but the lack of water here will kill us."

Poor Nations Suffer the Most

Around the world, millions of people like Da Antonio are feeling the force of a changing climate. As UN [United Nations] negotiations towards a global climate deal continue in Poznan, Poland, this week [December 2008], evidence is emerging of weather patterns in turmoil and the poorest nations disproportionately bearing the brunt of warming.

While rich countries at the talks seek to set up global carbon trading, using financial markets to tackle —and profit from— climate change, poor countries want justice. They are seeking environmental justice: money to adapt their economies to climate changes they did not cause, and technology and resources to allow them to escape poverty while preserving their forests and ecosystems.

The fast and unpredictable shifts in weather are not threats for the future, but happening right now.

The fast and unpredictable shifts in weather are not threats for the future, but happening right now. "The frequency of heatwaves and heavy precipitation is increasing; cyclones are becoming more frequent and intense; more areas are being affected by droughts; and flooding is now more serious," says Sheridan Bartlett, a researcher with the International Institute for Environment and Development in a new study looking at the effects of climate change on children.

"Increasingly unpredictable weather now affects hundreds of millions of farmers, resulting in food and water shortages, more illnesses and water-borne diseases, malnutrition, soil erosion, and disruption to water supplies," she says. Such changes confound the received wisdom of how to live on the land.

North-east Brazil has always known droughts, but they are becoming longer and more frequent, say scientists and farmers. "Climate change is biting. It is much hotter than it used to be and it stays hotter for longer. The rain has become more sporadic. It comes at different times of the year now and farmers cannot tell when to plant," says Lindon Carlos, an agronomist with Brazilian group Acev.

Brazilian scientists have recorded changes in the lifecycles of plants, greater oscillations in temperature and more water shortages, all consistent with the UN Intergovernmental Panel on Climate Change (IPCC) predictions of a devastating 3–4C [degree Celsius] rise in temperatures within 60 years if climate change is not halted. "All the research points to it becoming drier [in north-east Brazil]. In the last 30 years temperatures have risen by 1C. There is more very heavy rainfall over short periods and more evaporation," says Eneida Cavalcanti, a desertification specialist at the Joaquim Nabuco Foundation in Recife.

Cyclones Strike More Often

On the other side of the world, the changing climate is wreaking havoc in a different way on low-lying and populous Bangladesh. There, government meteorologists this year reported a 10% increase in intensity and frequency in major cyclones hitting the country—two of the most powerful cyclones ever recorded have hit the country in the last three years.

"We are getting too much water in the rainy season and too little in the dry season. All this has implications for food security," says Raja Debashish Roy, Bangladesh's environment minister.

"We are learning about climate change," said Anawarul Islam, chair of the Deara district of about 2,500 people in the far south of the county. "This village is experiencing more rainfall and flooding every year. It has led to more homeless people and more conflict."

The balmy Caribbean is also being churned up with increasing frequency and ferocity.

"It's far warmer now," says one villager, Selina. "We do not feel cold in the rainy season. We used to need blankets, but now we don't. There is extreme uncertainty of weather. It makes it very hard to farm and we cannot plan. We have to be more reactive. The storms are increasing and the tides now come right up to our houses."

The balmy Caribbean is also being churned up with increasing frequency and ferocity. This year [2008], the region experienced eight hurricanes and five major hurricanes, the second highest ever, and the hurricane season lasted a record five months.

"A warmer climate poses in some cases insurmountable challenges to the region. We face more hurricanes, coral bleaching and flooding," said Neville Trotz, science adviser to the Caribbean community climate change centre.

Across the Atlantic, in Africa, the theme unfolds further: climate change turning already bad situations in poor countries into potential catastrophe, and driving people to absolute poverty. Alexandre Tique, at Mozambique's national meteorological institute, says: "Analysis of the temperature data gathered in our provincial capitals, where we have meteorological stations that have kept continuous data over the years, shows a clear increase in temperature. Extreme events are becoming more frequent. We now see many more tropical cyclones that bring flooding, destruction and loss of lives."

Droughts Threaten Many Farmers

Other African communities are suffering. In the village of Chikani, in Zambia, the farmers last year prepared their fields for planting in November, as they have always done, but the rains were very late for the third year running.

"We waited, but the first drop didn't fall till December 20. After a day, the rains stopped. Three weeks later, it started to rain again. But then it stopped again after a few days. Since then, we have had no rain. We have never known anything like this before," says Julius Njame.

From the plains of Africa, to mountaintop Nepal, there is no respite from the weather in flux. Villages like Ketbari expect a small flood to wash off the hills every decade or so, now they seem to be annual and getting more serious.

"We always used to have a little rain each month, but now when there is rain it's very different. It's more concentrated and intense. It means that crop yields are going down," says Tekmadur Majsi, whose lands have been progressively washed away by the Trishuli river.

Many lakes in Nepal and neighbouring Bhutan, which collect glacier meltwater, are said by the UN to be growing so rapidly that they could burst their banks.

Nepalese villagers observe the minutiae of a changing climate. Some say that forest pigs now farrow earlier, others that some types of rice and cucumber will no longer grow where they used to. The common thread is that the days are hotter, some trees now flower twice a year and the raindrops are getting bigger.

The anecdotal observations of farmers are backed by scientists who are recording in Nepal some of the fastest increases in temperatures and rainfall anywhere in the world. Many lakes in Nepal and neighbouring Bhutan, which collect glacier meltwater, are said by the UN to be growing so rapidly that they could burst their banks.

Glaciers Are Disappearing

Melting glaciers are creating anxiety about water supplies across the Earth. In Tajikistan, at current rates of change, thousands of small glaciers will have disappeared completely by 2050, causing more water to flow in spring followed by what is expected to be a disastrous decline of river flow in most rivers. In Peru, temperature increases have led to a 22% reduction in the total area of its glaciers in the last 35 years.

The developing nations on the climate frontline will argue strongly in Poznan that rich countries should pay to help them adapt to climate change. But development groups such as Oxfam and Tearfund say that almost all the money pledged so far has come out of existing aid funds. With a worldwide recession, many analysts expect rich countries to resist paying more.

The UN has established two funds—the Least Developed Countries and Special Climate Change funds—to raise money for the poorest countries to adapt, but the [major government-ments forum] G8 countries have only pledged $6bn [billion] (£4bn). All the money is to be diverted from existing aid money.

"Every [official development assistance] dollar that goes to climate adaptation would mean a dollar less for health and education [programmes] in developing countries," said Antonio Hill, a senior policy adviser at Oxfam.

The scale of what is needed for adaptation is immense. Bangladesh says it needs £250m [million] over three years to adapt, Ethiopia £450m, and other countries similar amounts. Development groups estimate that a minimum $50bn a year is needed worldwide.

"The resources currently available for adaptation are grossly inadequate to meet the needs of the least developed countries who bear the brunt of increased climate variability and unpredictability resulting from climate change," said Bangladesh's finance minister, Mirza Azizul Islam.

Back in north-east Brazil, the Pernambuco state environment minister, Aloysio Coasta, says: "In 20 years' time we could be a desert region. In some communities there are no young people left at all. This is an emergency. Food production is going down in many areas."

Joao da Antonio's wife, Luiza, is resigned to becoming a "drought widow". Clearly distressed, she says: "If there is no water, then he must leave."

5

Global Warming Can't Explain All Disasters

Joel Achenbach

Joel Achenbach is a reporter on The Washington Post's *national staff.*

Global warming is a serious issue, but it is blamed wrongly for each and every current disaster. The main problem is not that climate change produces weather disasters, but that mankind is overfishing, over-farming, polluting, and destroying the planet. Furthermore, as wildfires and hurricanes show, people are building their homes in high-risk areas and ignoring common sense. We need to fight global warming, but it is only one of many issues contributing to Earth's disasters.

We're heading into the heart of hurricane season, and any day now, a storm will barrel toward the United States, inspiring all the TV weather reporters to find a beach where they can lash themselves to a palm tree. We can be certain of two things: First, we'll be told that the wind is blowing very hard and the surf is up. Second, some expert will tell us that this storm might be a harbinger of global warming.

Somewhere along the line, global warming became the explanation for everything. Right-thinking people are not supposed to discuss any meteorological or geophysical event—a hurricane, a wildfire, a heat wave, a drought, a flood, a blizzard, a tornado, a lightning strike, an unfamiliar breeze, a strange tingling on the neck—without immediately invoking the climate crisis. It causes earthquakes, plagues and backyard gardening disappointments. Weird fungus on your tomato plants? *Classic* sign of global warming.

You are permitted to note, as a parenthetical, that no single weather calamity can be ascribed with absolute certainty (roll your eyes here to signal the exasperating fussiness of scientists) to what humans are doing to the atmosphere. But your tone will make it clear that this is just legalese, like the fine-print warnings on the flip side of a Lipitor [a drug for lowering blood cholesterol] ad.

Some people are impatient with even a token amount of equivocation. A science writer for *Newsweek* recently flat-out declared that this year's [2008] floods in the Midwest were the result of climate change, and in the process, she derided the wishy-washy climatologists who couldn't quite bring themselves to reach that conclusion (they "trip over themselves to absolve global warming").

Well, gosh, I dunno. Equivocation isn't a sign of cognitive weakness. Uncertainty is intrinsic to the scientific process, and sometimes you have to have the courage to stand up and say, "Maybe."

Seems to me that it's inherently impossible to *prove* a causal connection between climate and weather—they're just two different things. Moreover, the evidence for man-made climate change is solid enough that it doesn't need to be bolstered by iffy claims. Rigorous science is the best weapon for persuading the public that this is a real problem that requires bold action. "Weather alarmism" gives ammunition to global-warming deniers. They're happy to fight on that turf, since they can say that a year with relatively few hurricanes (or a cold snap when you don't expect it) proves that global warming is a myth. As science writer John Tierney put it in the *New York Times* earlier this year, weather alarmism "leaves climate politics at the mercy of the weather."

There's an ancillary issue here: Global warming threatens to suck all the oxygen out of any discussion of the environment. We wind up giving too little attention to habitat destruction, overfishing, invasive species tagging along with global trade and so on. You don't need a climate model to detect that big oil spill in the Mississippi. That "dead zone" in the Gulf of Mexico—an oxygen-starved region the size of Massachusetts—isn't caused by global warming, but by all that fertilizer spread on Midwest cornfields.

It's inherently impossible to prove a causal connection between climate and weather—they're just two different things.

Some folks may actually get the notion that the planet will be safe if we all just start driving Priuses [hybrid-electric cars made by Toyota]. But even if we cured ourselves of our addiction to fossil fuels and stabilized the planet's climate, we'd still have an environmental crisis on our hands. Our fundamental problem is that—now it's my chance to sound hysterical—humans are a species out of control. We've been hellbent on wrecking our environment pretty much since the day we figured out how to make fire.

This caused *that*: It would be nice if climate and weather were that simple.

But "one can only speak rationally about odds," Kerry Emanuel, a climatologist at the Massachusetts Institute of Technology who has studied hurricanes and climate change, told me last week [July 2008]. "Global warming increases the probabilities of floods and strong hurricanes, and that is all that you can say."

Emanuel's research shows that in the past 25 years, there's been an uptick in the number of strong storms, though not necessarily in the number of hurricanes overall. Climate models show that a 1-degree Celsius rise in sea-surface temperatures should intensify top winds by about 5 percent, which corresponds to a 15 percent increase in destructive power. The tropical Atlantic sea surface has warmed by 0.6 degrees Celsius in the past half-century.

At my request, Emanuel ran a computer program to see how much extra energy Hurricane Katrina had because of increases in sea-surface temperature. His conclusion: Katrina's winds were about 2 percent stronger in the Gulf, and not significantly stronger at landfall. Maybe climate change was a factor in generating such a storm, or in the amount of moisture it carried, but the catastrophe that Katrina caused in New Orleans can more plausibly be attributed to civil engineers who built inadequate levees, city planning that let neighborhoods materialize below sea level and [George W.] Bush administration officials who didn't do such a heckuva job.

Let's go back to those Iowa floods. Humans surely contributed to the calamity: Farmland in the Midwest has been plumbed with drainage pipes; streams have been straightened; most of the state's wetlands have been engineered out of existence; land set aside for conservation is being put back into corn production to meet the demands of the ethanol boom. This is a landscape that's practically begging to have 500-year floods every decade.

Was climate change a factor in the floods? Maybe. A recent report from the National Oceanic and Atmospheric Administration [NOAA] said that heavier downpours are more likely in a warming world. Thomas Karl, a NOAA scientist, says that there has been a measurable increase in water vapor over parts of the United States and more precipitation in the Midwest.

But tree-ring data indicate that the state has gone through a cycle of increasing and decreasing rainfall for hundreds of years. The downpours this year weren't that unusual, according to Harry J. Hillaker Jr., the Iowa state meteorologist. "The intensity has not really been excessive on a short-term scale," he said. "We're not seeing three-inch-an-hour rainfall amounts."

Rest assured, we may find ways to ruin the planet even before the worst effects of global warming kick in.

This will be a wet year (as was last year), but Iowa may not set a rainfall record. The wettest year on record was 1993. The second wettest: 1881. The third wettest: 1902.

Iowa is an awkward place to talk about global warming, because the state has actually been a bit cooler in the summer than it was in the first half of the 20th century. Hillaker says the widespread shift to annual plants (corn and soybeans) and away from perennial grasses has altered the climate. The 10 hottest summers in Iowa have been, in order, 1936, 1934, 1901, 1988, 1983, 1931, 1921, 1955, 1933 and 1913. Talk about extreme weather: One day in 1936, Iowa set a state record with a high temperature of 117 degrees. And no one blamed it on global warming.

Rest assured, we may find ways to ruin the planet even before the worst effects of global warming kick in. The thing that gets you in the end is rarely the thing you're paying attention to.

The basic problem is that there are so many of us now. Four centuries ago, there were about 500 million people on Earth. Today there are that many, plus 6 billion. We're rapidly heading toward 9 billion. Conservatives say that we just need to focus on maintaining free markets and let everything sort itself out through the miracle of the invisible hand. But the political tide is turning against unfettered free markets and toward greater regulation. Climate-change policy is part of that: Somehow we've got to embed environmental effects into the cost of energy sources, consumer goods and so on. The market approach by itself has let us down.

Viewed broadly, it appears that humans are environment-destroying creatures by nature. The notion of the prelapsarian era in which we lived in perfect harmony with nature has been effectively shattered by such scientists as Jared Diamond, the author of *Collapse*, and Tim Flannery, who wrote *The Future Eaters*. If everything gets simplified and reduced to a global-warming narrative, we'll be unable to see the trees for the forest.

[In July 2008], we saw reports of more wildfires in California. Sure as night follows day, people will lay some of the blame on climate change.

Consider the June [2008] issue of *Scientific American*, where you'll find a photograph of a parched lake, the mud baked into the kind of desiccated tiles that scream "drought." The caption says: "Climate shift to unprecedentedly dry weather, along with diversion of water for irrigation, has converted this former reservoir in China's Minqin County into desert."

Um . . . "this former reservoir?" Look closely, and you can see concrete walls in the background. This is not a natural place: It's a manufactured landscape. Here's a wild guess: This part of China is an environmental disaster that has very little to do with climate change and very much to do with high population and intensifying agriculture.

Last week [in July 2008], we saw reports of more wildfires in California. Sure as night follows day, people will lay some of the blame on climate change. But there's also the minor matter of people building homes in wildfire-susceptible forests, overgrown with vegetation due to decades of fire suppression. That's like pitching a tent on the railroad tracks.

The message that needs to be communicated to these people is: "Your problem is not global warming. Your problem is that you're nuts."

You should definitely worry about global warming. But you don't need to worry about global warming when your house is on fire.

6

Man-Made Climate Change Might Drown Whole Cities

UN Office for the Coordination of Humanitarian Affairs

The UN (United Nations) Office for the Coordination of Humanitarian Affairs (OCHA) seeks to coordinate effective and principled humanitarian action to help prevent and prepare for disasters.

Dhaka, the capital of Bangladesh—plus as many as 3,000 other cities worldwide—might soon face severe floods caused by global warming and a rise in sea levels. Urban growth and an increasing slum population have seen housing spread in unsafe areas, and many districts are ill-prepared for natural disasters. Global warmth threatens to kill off many species, induce worse weather disasters, and influence catastrophic consequences for poorer nations.

People in Dhaka, the capital of Bangladesh, prefer to commute in three-wheeled autorickshaws, taxis and buses that run on compressed natural gas (CNG), in their bid to slow down global warming.

CNG produces a lower level of greenhouse gases and is an environmentally cleaner alternative to petrol. Dhaka's residents are among the most vulnerable to global warming and don't want to become "climate terrorists".

The city is among more than 3,000 identified by the UN [United Nations]-Habitat's State of the World's Cities 2008/09

UN Office for the Coordination of Humanitarian Affairs, "Climate Change May Drown Cities," *Irin News*, October 24, 2008. Reproduced by permission.

as facing the prospect of sea level rise and surge-induced flooding. The report warns policymakers, planners and the world at large that few coastal cities will be spared the effects of global warming.

Asia accounts for more than half the most vulnerable cities, followed by Latin America and the Caribbean (27 percent) and Africa (15 percent); two-thirds of the cities are in Europe, and almost one-fifth of all cities in North America are in Low Elevation Coastal Zones (LECZ).

During the 1900s, sea levels rose by an estimated 17cm; global mean projections for sea level rise between 1990 and 2080 range from 22cm to 34cm, according to the UN-Habitat researchers.

Rising Sea Levels Could Spell Disaster

The report points out that by 2070, urban populations in river delta cities, such as Dhaka, Kolkata (India), Yangon (Myanmar), and Hai Phong (on the coast near Hanoi in Vietnam), which already experience a high risk of flooding, will join the group of populations most exposed to this danger. Port cities in Bangladesh, China, Thailand, Vietnam, and India will have joined the ranks of cities whose assets are most at risk.

African coastal cities that could be severely affected by rising sea levels include Abidjan (Cote d'Ivoire), Accra (Ghana), Alexandria (Egypt), Algiers (Algeria), Cape Town (South Africa), Casablanca (Morocco), Dakar (Senegal), Dar es Salaam (Tanzania), Djibouti (Djibouti), Durban (South Africa), Freetown (Sierra Leone), Lagos (Nigeria), Libreville (Gabon), Lome (Togo), Luanda (Angola), Maputo (Mozambique), Mombasa (Kenya), Port Louis (Mauritius), and Tunis (Tunisia).

Dhaka is wedged between huge rivers like the Ganges and the Brahmaputra, with hundreds of tributaries swollen with increasing glacial melt from the Himalayan ranges as a result of soaring global temperatures.

"The elevation in Dhaka ranges between two and 13 metres above sea level, which means that even a slight rise in sea level is likely to engulf large parts of the city. Moreover, high urban growth rates and high urban densities have already made Dhaka more susceptible to human-induced environmental disasters," said the UN-Habitat report.

"With an urban growth rate of more than four percent annually, Dhaka, which already hosts more than 13 million people, is one of the fastest growing cities in Southern Asia, and is projected to accommodate more than 20 million by 2025.

"The sheer number of people living in the city means that the negative consequences of climate change are likely to be felt by a large number of people, especially the urban poor who live in flood-prone and water-logged areas."

A total 634 million people in the world live in LECZ that lie at or below 10 metres above sea level, according to a recent report, "Planet Prepare," by World Vision, a Christian relief, development and advocacy organisation. Although LECZ constitute only two percent of the earth's landmass, they contain 10 percent of its population and have a higher rate of urbanisation than the rest of the world.

Dhaka's solutions should also take into consideration unresolved development problems, such as the growing slum population, which has doubled in the last decade and shows no signs of abating.

Ban Ki-moon, Secretary-General of the UN, notes his concern about the prospect of large-scale devastation in his foreword to the UN-Habitat report, saying: "Cities embody some of society's most pressing challenges, from pollution and disease to unemployment and lack of adequate shelter. But cities are also venues where rapid, dramatic change is not just possible but expected."

Preparations for the Next Disaster

Dhaka is preparing for flood protection. The government, prompted by frequent flooding in the 1980s, has already completed embankments, reinforced concrete walls and pumping stations in the most densely populated part of the city.

The UN report cautioned that Dhaka's solutions should also take into consideration unresolved development problems, such as the growing slum population, which has doubled in the last decade and shows no signs of abating.

The World Vision report pointed out that other urban centres not physically challenged by global warming would also face tremendous challenges, with the possible influx of "environmental refugees" from affected cities.

The Intergovernmental Panel on Climate Change (IPCC) has urged global greenhouse gas emission reductions of 50 percent to 85 percent by 2050, based on 2000 emissions, to avoid a 2°Celsius increase in global mean temperature.

Such an increase is expected to destroy 30 percent to 40 percent of all known species, generate bigger, fiercer and more frequent heat waves and droughts, and more intense weather events like floods and cyclones.

The IPCC and activists have called on the global community to focus on preventing global warming from crossing the perilous 2°C threshold, which requires keeping atmospheric carbon dioxide (CO_2) concentrations below 350ppm (parts per million).

"The problem is, they [concentrations] already stand at 385ppm (2008), rising by 2ppm annually," said the World Vision report. "Since there are no rewind buttons for running down emitted greenhouse gas stocks, implicational reasoning suggests immediate and stringent emissions cuts."

Eminent scientists, such as James E. Hansen, who heads NASA's Goddard Institute for Space Studies, are warning that even the 2-degree threshold may likely not be safe enough to avoid "global disaster".

7

Global Warming Is a Sign of a New Ice Age

Gregory Fegel

Gregory Fegel is a writer and blogger.

The current debate about climate change focuses on Anthropogenic Global Warming (AGW) and, consequently, greenhouse gases are blamed for many natural disasters. Yet according to the Milankovich theory, which takes into account the entire history of Earth, we are on the brink of a new Ice Age. Most researchers focus on short-term effects, rather than the bigger picture, and ignore the threat of large parts of the globe becoming uninhabitable.

The earth is now on the brink of entering another Ice Age, according to a large and compelling body of evidence from within the field of climate science. Many sources of data which provide our knowledge base of long-term climate change indicate that the warm, twelve thousand year-long Holocene period will rather soon be coming to an end, and then the earth will return to Ice Age conditions for the next 100,000 years.

Ice cores, ocean sediment cores, the geologic record, and studies of ancient plant and animal populations all demonstrate a regular cyclic pattern of Ice Age glacial maximums which each last about 100,000 years, separated by intervening warm interglacials, each lasting about 12,000 years.

Gregory Fegel, "Earth on the Brink of an Ice Age," *Pravda.ru*, January 11, 2009. Reproduced by permission.

Most of the long-term climate data collected from various sources also shows a strong correlation with the three astronomical cycles which are together known as the Milankovich cycles. The three Milankovich cycles include the tilt of the earth, which varies over a 41,000 year period; the shape of the earth's orbit, which changes over a period of 100,000 years; and the Precession of the Equinoxes, also known as the earth's 'wobble', which gradually rotates the direction of the earth's axis over a period of 26,000 years. According to the Milankovich theory of Ice Age causation, these three astronomical cycles, each of which effects the amount of solar radiation which reaches the earth, act together to produce the cycle of cold Ice Age maximums and warm interglacials.

Most of the long-term climate data collected from various sources also shows a strong correlation with the three astronomical cycles which are together known as the Milankovich cycles.

Research Points to a New Ice Age

Elements of the astronomical theory of Ice Age causation were first presented by the French mathematician Joseph Adhemar in 1842, it was developed further by the English prodigy Joseph Croll in 1875, and the theory was established in its present form by the Serbian mathematician Milutin Milankovich in the 1920s and 30s. In 1976 the prestigious journal *Science* published a landmark paper by John Imbrie, James Hays, and Nicholas Shackleton entitled "Variations in the Earth's orbit: Pacemaker of the Ice Ages," which described the correlation which the trio of scientist/authors had found between the climate data obtained from ocean sediment cores and the patterns of the astronomical Milankovich cycles. Since the late 1970s, the Milankovich theory has remained the predominant theory to account for Ice Age causation among climate scientists, and hence the Milankovich theory is always described in textbooks of climatology and in encyclopaedia articles about the Ice Ages.

In their 1976 paper Imbrie, Hays, and Shackleton wrote that their own climate forecasts, which were based on sea-sediment cores and the Milankovich cycles, ". . . must be qualified in two ways. First, they apply only to the natural component of future climatic trends—and not to anthropogenic effects such as those due to the burning of fossil fuels. Second, they describe only the long-term trends, because they are linked to orbital variations with periods of 20,000 years and longer. Climatic oscillations at higher frequencies are not predicted . . . the results indicate that the long-term trend over the next 20,000 years is towards extensive Northern Hemisphere glaciation and cooler climate."

The Fear of Global Warming

During the 1970s the famous American astronomer Carl Sagan and other scientists began promoting the theory that 'greenhouse gasses' such as carbon dioxide, or CO_2, produced by human industries could lead to catastrophic global warming. Since the 1970s the theory of 'anthropogenic [derived from human activities] global warming' (AGW) has gradually become accepted as fact by most of the academic establishment, and their acceptance of AGW has inspired a global movement to encourage governments to make pivotal changes to prevent the worsening of AGW.

The 'hockey stick' graph shows an acute upward spike in global temperatures which began during the 1970s and continued through the winter of 2006/07.

The central piece of evidence that is cited in support of the AGW theory is the famous 'hockey stick' graph which was presented by Al Gore in his 2006 film *An Inconvenient Truth.*

The 'hockey stick' graph shows an acute upward spike in global temperatures which began during the 1970s and continued through the winter of 2006/07. However, this warming trend was interrupted when the winter of 2007/8 delivered the deepest snow cover to the Northern Hemisphere since 1966 and the coldest temperatures since 2001. It now appears that the current Northern Hemisphere winter of 2008/09 will probably equal or surpass the winter of 2007/08 for both snow depth and cold temperatures.

The main flaw in the AGW theory is that its proponents focus on evidence from only the past one thousand years at most, while ignoring the evidence from the past million years—evidence which is essential for a true understanding of climatology. The data from paleoclimatology [study of climate change taken on the scale of the entire history of Earth] provides us with an alternative and more credible explanation for the recent global temperature spike, based on the natural cycle of Ice Age maximums and interglacials.

Looking into the Past for Clues

In 1999 the British journal *Nature* published the results of data derived from glacial ice cores collected at the Russia's Vostok station in Antarctica during the 1990s. The Vostok ice core data includes a record of global atmospheric temperatures, atmospheric CO_2 and other greenhouse gases, and airborne particulates starting from 420,000 years ago and continuing through history up to our present time.

The graph of the Vostok ice core data shows that the Ice Age maximums and the warm interglacials occur within a regular cyclic pattern, the graph-line of which is similar to the rhythm of a heartbeat on an electrocardiogram tracing. The Vostok data graph also shows that changes in global CO_2 levels lag behind global temperature changes by about eight hundred years. What that indicates is that global temperatures precede or cause global CO_2 changes, and not the reverse. In other words, increasing atmospheric CO_2 is not causing global temperature to rise; instead the natural cyclic increase in global temperature is causing global CO_2 to rise.

The reason that global CO_2 levels rise and fall in response to the global temperature is because cold water is capable of retaining more CO_2 than warm water. That is why carbonated beverages loose their carbonation or CO_2, when stored in a warm environment. We store our carbonated soft drinks, wine, and beer in a cool place to prevent them from loosing their 'fizz', which is a feature of their carbonation, or CO_2 content. The earth is currently warming as a result of the natural Ice Age cycle, and as the oceans get warmer, they release increasing amounts of CO_2 into the atmosphere.

We should already be eight hundred years into the coming Ice Age before global CO_2 levels begin to drop in response to the increased chilling of the world's oceans.

CO_2 Levels Will Continue to Rise

Because the release of CO_2 by the warming oceans lags behind the changes in the earth's temperature, we should expect to see global CO_2 levels continue to rise for another eight hundred years after the end of the earth's current Interglacial warm period. We should already be eight hundred years into the coming Ice Age before global CO_2 levels begin to drop in response to the increased chilling of the world's oceans.

The Vostok ice core data graph reveals that global CO_2 levels regularly rose and fell in a direct response to the natural cycle of Ice Age minimums and maximums during the past four hundred and twenty thousand years. Within that natural cycle, about every 110,000 years global temperatures, followed by global CO_2 levels, have peaked at approximately the same levels which they are at today.

Today we are again at the peak, and near to the end, of a warm interglacial, and the earth is now due to enter the next Ice Age. If we are lucky, we may have a few years to prepare for it. The Ice Age will return, as it always has, in its regular and natural cycle, with or without any influence from the effects of AGW.

The AGW theory is based on data that are drawn from a ridiculously narrow span of time and it demonstrates a wanton disregard for the 'big picture' of long-term climate change. The data from paleoclimatology, including ice cores, sea sediments, geology, paleobotany and zoology, indicate that we are on the verge of entering another Ice Age, and the data also show that severe and lasting climate change can occur within only a few years. While concern over the dubious threat of Anthropogenic Global Warming continues to distract the attention of people throughout the world, the very real threat of the approaching and inevitable Ice Age, which will render large parts of the Northern Hemisphere uninhabitable, is being foolishly ignored.

8

Disasters Are Far From Natural

Sharon Begley

Sharon Begley writes a bi-weekly column, essays, and cover stories for Newsweek.

While disasters might be natural, the horrific consequences of, for example, hurricanes, are often anything but. All over the American South, development booms have put people in harms way, and it is often the poorer populations who live in the most affected areas. Even measures to prevent damage, such as maintaining the New Orleans levees, have negative impacts on the environment, and, ultimately, on the disastrous effects of storms. City planners and government officials can't afford to ignore man-made disasters any longer, if they want to prevent another Katrina.

While storms such as Hurricane Katrina [August 2005] are sometimes called an act of God or a natural disaster, the devastation they leave behind is not. Some scientists believe even the storms themselves could be at least partly man-made.

As Theodore Steinberg argues, God is getting a bum rap. "This is an unnatural disaster if ever there was one, not an act of God," says Professor Steinberg, an environmental historian at Case Western Reserve University, Cleveland. "If the potential for mass death and destruction from extreme weather existed anywhere in the U.S., it existed in New Orleans."

In his 2000 book "Acts of God: The Unnatural History of Natural Disaster in America," Prof. Steinberg documented how much of the toll from "natural" disasters, from the 1886 Charleston earthquake to 1990s hurricanes, has been exacerbated by human actions.

Man-Made Disasters

The temporary lull in hurricane activity in Florida, from 1969 to 1989, spurred a reckless building boom, for example, putting billions of dollars worth of condos and hotels within reach of storm surges, notes Roger Pielke Jr., of the University of Colorado, Boulder. The Great Miami Hurricane of 1926 would have caused an estimated $90 billion damage had it occurred in 2000, he calculated. It caused just over $1 billion, in today's dollars.

It isn't only hurricanes whose destructiveness has been increased by human actions. Tornadoes turn mobile homes into matchsticks (one of Prof. Steinberg's first jobs was at a New York brokerage firm, where he followed the trailer-home industry). From 1981 to 1997, he found, more than one-third of all deaths from tornadoes occurred among people living in mobile homes; federal regulations didn't require them to withstand high winds, and a 1974 statute actually pre-empted stricter state standards with more lax federal ones.

Throughout the South and Midwest, mobile-home communities and poor neighborhoods are also much more likely to be sited in flood plains.

In New Orleans, the worst-hit parishes were the lower-income ones. But the city also ignored the power of nature.

In New Orleans, the worst-hit parishes were the lower-income ones. But the city also ignored the power of nature. More than one million acres of Louisiana's coastal wetlands or

1,900 square miles, have been lost since 1930, due to development and the construction of levees and canals. Barrier islands and stands of tupelo and cypress also vanished. All of them absorb some of the energy and water from storm surges, which, more than the rain falling from the sky, caused the current calamity. "If these had been in place, at least some of the energy in the storm surge would have been dissipated," says geologist Jeffrey Mount of the University of California, Davis. "This is a self-inflicted wound."

Studies estimate that for every square mile of wetlands lost storm surges rise by one foot.

Levees Exacerbated the Disaster

Leaving aside whether the levees that broke in New Orleans could have been better constructed, their very existence contributed to the disaster. Built to keep the city from being flooded by the Mississippi, they also keep the Big Muddy from depositing silt to replenish marshes and the river's delta, as do projects that direct the river's water and sediment out to sea to create a deep shipping channel.

As the seas and air warm, there is more evaporation, which fuels storms, and more energy available to pump them up.

The result is that much of New Orleans fell below sea level. Combined with the dredging to build canals, "the Gulf of Mexico is a lot closer to New Orleans than it was when Hurricane Betsy ripped through in 1965," says Prof. Steinberg. Now the gulf is in the city.

The ultimate question is whether Katrina's power reflects human-caused global warming, or is at minimum a harbinger of the kinds of storms we can expect in a warmer world.

No single freak storm can be attributed to global climate trends. But for hurricanes to form, the surface temperature in the tropical Atlantic must exceed about 80° Fahrenheit. That is more likely in a warmer world.

The best science to date suggests the frequency of hurricanes doesn't reflect global warming. Straightforward physics, however, says their intensity might. As the seas and air warm, there is more evaporation, which fuels storms, and more energy available to pump them up. A new analysis by atmospheric physicist Kerry Emanuel of MIT [Massachusetts Institute of Technology] suggests the net power of tropical cyclones (hurricanes and Pacific typhoons), a combination of the energy they pack and how long they last, "has increased markedly since 1970."

The power of storms in the North Atlantic has tripled, while the power of those in the western North Pacific has more than doubled.

Similarly, a 2004 study from the Geophysical Fluid Dynamics Laboratory in Princeton, New Jersey, part of the National Oceanic and Atmospheric Administration, found that a warmer world is likely to deepen hurricanes' central pressure (a measure of their power) and intensify the rainfall they bring. Today's storms, the scientists write, "may be upstaged by even more intense hurricanes over the next century as the earth's climate is warmed by increasing levels of greenhouse gases in the atmosphere."

By continuing to blame weather extremes on random events, the "stuff happens" attitude, officials and city planners are ignoring their contributions to the disasters that have pummeled the planet and promise to become only worse.

9

Social Politics Decide What Events Become Disasters

Neil Smith

Neil Smith is Distinguished Professor of Anthropology and Geography at the City University of New York's (CUNY) Graduate Center. His most recent book is The Endgame of Globalization.

Disasters depend on where natural events happen, and so far, society has been ignoring signs of global warming that put places like New Orleans, La., or Venice, Italy, at great risk. Instead of preparing communities around the world for impending disasters, politicians have questioned obvious causes and done little or nothing to keep the population safe. Disasters are exploited by developers and politicians, who, after a tsunami or hurricane strikes, ensure that the poorer inhabitants do not return to their homes, and instead develop the space for profitable projects for the wealthy. But examples in the Caribbean show that storms don't have to be deadly and that, if local communities organize, disasters can be prevented.

It is generally accepted among environmental geographers that there is no such thing as a natural disaster. In every phase and aspect of a disaster—causes, vulnerability, preparedness, results and response, and reconstruction—the contours of disaster and the difference between who lives and who dies is to a greater or lesser extent a social calculus. Hurricane Katrina [August 2005] provides the most startling confirmation of that axiom. This is not simply an academic point

Neil Smith, "There's No Such Thing as a Natural Disaster," June 11, 2006. Reproduced by permission.

but a practical one, and it has everything to do with how societies prepare for and absorb natural events and how they can or should reconstruct afterward. It is difficult, so soon on the heels of such an unnecessarily deadly disaster, to be discompassionate, but it is important in the heat of the moment to put social science to work as a counterweight to official attempts to relegate Katrina to the historical dustbin of inevitable "natural" disasters.

The denial of the naturalness of disasters is in no way a denial of natural process.

Location Decides Whether or Not an Event Becomes a Disaster

First, causes. The denial of the naturalness of disasters is in no way a denial of natural process. Earthquakes, tsunamis, blizzards, droughts and hurricanes are certainly events of nature that require a knowledge of geophysics, physical geography or climatology to comprehend. Whether a natural event is a disaster or not depends ultimately, however, on its location. A large earthquake in the Hindu Kush [mountain system in Central Asia] may spawn no disaster whatsoever while the same intensity event in California could be a catastrophe. But even among climatic events, natural causes are not entirely divorced from the social. The world has recently experienced dramatic warming, which scientists increasingly attribute to airborne emissions of carbon, and around the world Katrina is widely seen as evidence of socially induced climatic change. Much as a single hurricane such as Katrina, even when followed by an almost equally intense Hurricane Rita, or even when embedded in a record 2005 season of Atlantic hurricanes, is not in itself conclusive evidence of humanly induced global warming. Yet it would be irresponsible to ignore such signals. The [George W.] Bush administration has done just that, and it is happy to attribute the dismal record of death and destruction on the Gulf Coast—perhaps 1200 lives by the latest counts—to an act of nature. It has proven itself not just oblivious but ideologically opposed to mounting scientific evidence of global warming and the fact that rising sea-levels make cities such as New Orleans, Venice [Italy], or Dacca [Bangladesh] immediately vulnerable to future calamity. Whatever the political tampering with science, the supposed "naturalness" of disasters here becomes an ideological camouflage for the social (and therefore preventable) dimensions of such disasters, covering for quite specific social interests.

Vulnerability, in turn, is highly differentiated; some people are much more vulnerable than others. Put bluntly, in many climates rich people tend to take the higher land, leaving to the poor and working class land more vulnerable to flooding and environmental pestilence. This is a trend not an iron clad generalization: oceanfront property marks a major exception in many places, and Bolivia's La Paz, where the wealthy live in the cooler valley below 13,000 feet, is another. In New Orleans, however, topographic gradients doubled as class and race gradients, and as the Katrina evacuation so tragically demonstrated, the better off had cars to get out, credit cards and bank accounts for emergency hotels and supplies, their immediate families likely had resources to support their evacuation, and the wealthier also had the insurance policies for rebuilding. Not just the market but successive administrations from the federal to the urban scale, made the poorest population in New Orleans most vulnerable. Since 2001, knowing that a catastrophic hurricane was likely and would in all probability devastate New Orleans, the Bush administration nonetheless opened hundreds of square miles of wetland to development on the grounds that the market knows best, and in the process eroded New Orleans' natural protection; and they cut the New Orleans Corps of Engineers budget by 80%, thus preventing pumping and levee improvements. At the same time, they syphoned resources toward tax cuts for the wealthy and a failed war in Iraq. Given the stunned amazement with which people around the world greeted images of a stranded African American populace in the deadly sewage pond of post-Katrina New Orleans, it is difficult not to agree with Illinois senator Barack Obama: "the people of New Orleans weren't just abandoned during the hurricane," but were "abandoned long ago."

The incompetence of preparations for Katrina, especially at the federal level, is well known.

Preparedness Can Avoid Disasters

After causes and vulnerability comes preparedness. The incompetence of preparations for Katrina, especially at the federal level, is well known. As soon as the hurricane hit Florida, almost three days before New Orleans, it was evident that this storm was far more dangerous than its wind speeds and intensity suggested. Meteorologists knew it would hit a multistate region but the Federal Emergency Management Agency (FEMA), overseen by a political appointee with no relevant experience and recently subordinated to the Homeland Security Administration, assumed business as usual. They sent only a quarter of available search and rescue teams to the region and no personnel to New Orleans until after the storm had passed. Yet more than a day before it hit, Katrina was described by the National Weather Service as a "hurricane with unprecedented strength" likely to make the targeted area "uninhabitable for weeks, perhaps longer." Days afterward, as the President hopped from photo-op to photo-op the White House, not given to listening to its scientists, seemed still not to understand the prescience of that warning or the dimensions of the disaster.

The results of Hurricane Katrina and responses to it are as of this writing still fresh in our memory but it is important to record some of the details so that the rawness of what transpired not be rubbed smooth by historical rewrite. The results can be assessed in thousands of lives unnecessarily lost, billions of dollars of property destroyed, local economies devastated and so forth, but that is only half the story. The images ricocheting around the world of a crippled United States, unconcerned or unable to protect its own population, receiving offers of aid from more than 100 countries, only reaffirmed for many the sense, already crystalizing from the debacle in Iraq, of a failing superpower. The level of survivors' amply televised anger, bodies floating in the background, shocked the world. Reporters were not "embedded" this time, and so the images were real, uncensored, and raw. As the true horror unfolded, the media were working without a script, and it took almost a week before pre-existing absorptive news narratives regained control. But by then it was too late. Distraught refugees, mostly African American, concluded that they were being left in the New Orleans Superdome and Convention Center to die; they pleaded for help, any help, as they angrily demanded to know why, if reporters could get in and out, they could not.

Unfortunately, shocking as it was, the tragedy of New Orleans is neither unique nor even especially unexpected, except perhaps in its scale.

Inadequate and Misguided Help

When the National Guard did arrive, it was quickly apparent that they were working under orders to control the city militarily and protect property rather than to bring aid to the desperate. Angry citizens, who waded through the fetid city looking for promised buses that never came, were prevented, at gunpoint, from getting out. "We are not turning the West Bank [a New Orleans suburb] into another Superdome," argued one suburban sheriff. Groups of refugees who tried to organize water, food and shelter collectively were also broken up at gunpoint by the national guard. Numerous victims reported being besieged and the National Guard was under orders not to distribute their own water. As late as four days after the hurricane hit New Orleans, with government aid still largely absent, President Bush advised refugees that they ought to rely on private charities such as the Salvation Army. When the first federal aid did come, stunned recipients opening boxes asked why they were being sent anthrax vaccine. "These are the boxes Homeland Security told us to send," came the reply.

Unfortunately, shocking as it was, the tragedy of New Orleans is neither unique nor even especially unexpected, except perhaps in its scale. The race and class dimensions of who escaped and who was victimized by this decidedly unnatural disaster not only could have been predicted, and was, but it follows a long history of like experiences. In 1976, a devastating earthquake eventually killed 23,000 people in Guatemala and made 1.5 million people homeless. I say "eventually," because the vast majority of deaths were not the direct result of the physical event itself but played out in the days and weeks that followed. Massive international relief flooded into Guatemala but it was not funneled to the most affected and neediest peasants, who eventually came to call the disaster a "classquake." In communities surrounding the Indian Ocean, ravaged by the tsunami of December 2004, the class and ethnic fissures of the old societies are re-etched deeper and wider by the patterns of response and reconstruction. There, "reconstruction" forcibly prevents local fishermen from re-establishing their livelihoods, planning instead to secure the oceanfront for wealthy tourists. Locals increasingly call the reconstruction effort the "second tsunami." In New Orleans there are already murmurings of Katrina as "Hurricane Bush." It is not only in the so-called Third World, we can now see, that one's chances of surviving a disaster are more than anything dependent on one's race, ethnicity and social class.

Protecting Only the Wealthy

At all phases, up to and including reconstruction, disasters don't simply flatten landscapes, washing them smooth. Rather they deepen and erode the ruts of social difference they encounter. Within a matter of days, with bodies still uncollected and before the death toll was even approximately known, discussion in the press turned to the opportunity represented by the laying bare of New Orleans. With an estimated half million people excluded from the city, FEMA began organizing mobile home parks to accommodate as many as 130,000 refugee families in far flung state parks, boy scout camps, any plausible tract of vacant land far from the city. On the face of it, this might be a reasonable strategy, except that one has to invest a lot of faith to imagine that the first item of business in New Orleans, with federal funding from the staunchly pro-market Bush administration, will be to reconstruct public housing so that those most in need can return to the city. Already, in the interlude between Katrina and the reflooding wrought by Hurricane Rita, businesses and homeowners were the privileged who were allowed back through military cordons into the city. It is far more likely therefore that working class and African American New Orleanians will be held on the outskirts for months and years on the grounds that they have no home to go back to, and in the hope or expectation that they will simply disperse in frustration.

In fact, many evacuees from hurricanes Charley and Ivan in 2004 remain in trailer parks in Florida. And neo-conservative *New York Times* editorialist David Brooks wasted no time arguing that "people who lack middle-class skills" should not be allowed to resettle the city: "If we just put up new buildings and allow the same people to move back into their old neighborhoods, then urban New Orleans will become just as run down as before." If it were true that the character of neighborhoods depended first and foremost on who moved into them there might be some truth in this. But if, as several generations of urban theory now argues, the fate of a neighborhood has as much if not more to do with how capital (public or private) invests in a neighborhood (and how it also disinvests), then the spotlight should be less on blaming the victims of this dreadful disaster than on the motives of capital investors. Congressional Representative Richard Baker of Baton Rouge provides little solace in this regard. "We finally cleaned up public housing in New Orleans," chuckled an unguarded Baker. "We couldn't do it, but God did."

Meanwhile, with many of the dead still unaccounted for, developers descended on New Orleans with wallets bulging and chops smacking.

Developers Sense Opportunity

The final lesson of environmental geography concerning disasters is that far from flattening the social differences, disaster reconstruction invariably cuts deeper the ruts and grooves of social oppression and exploitation. And so, while abolishing competition by giving no-bid contracts to some of the same companies that operate in Iraq—Bechtel, Fluor Corp., Haliburton—the Bush administration has mandated cutthroat competition among desperate workers by suspending the federal law that requires federal contractors to pay at least the prevailing local wage. Meanwhile, with many of the dead still unaccounted for, developers descended on New Orleans with wallets bulging and chops smacking. In anticipation that the city will be rebuilt with higher and better levees and with many fewer working class and African Americans, New Orleans two weeks after Katrina already looked like a developers' gold rush. These people, these developers and these corporations, say many New Orleanians, are the "true looters." By contrast, those displaced, with no private property to reclaim, face lower wages, escalating costs for scarce housing, and as the initial sympathy wears away, increased stigmatization.

When President Bush insists that "out of New Orleans is going to come that great city again," it is difficult to believe that good quality, secure and affordable social housing is what this administration has in mind. Wholesale gentrification at a scale as yet unseen in the United States is the more likely outcome. After the Bush hurricane, the poor, African American and working class people who evacuated will not be welcomed back to New Orleans, which will in all likelihood be rebuilt as a tourist magnet with a Disneyfied BigEasyVille oozing even more manufactured authenticity than the surviving French Quarter nearby.

The Kyoto protocols were far from perfect but they represented a lowest common denominator in fighting global warming that the US would not even sign onto.

We can look back and identify any number of individual decisions taken and not taken that made this hurricane such a social disaster. But the larger picture is more than the sum of its parts. It is not a radical conclusion that the dimensions of the Katrina disaster owe in large part not just to the actions of this or that local or federal administration but the operation of a capitalist market more broadly, especially in its neoliberal garb. The refusal to tackle global warming is rooted in the global power of the petroleum and energy corporations which fear for their profits and which, not coincidentally, represent the social class roots of the Bush administration's power; the New Orleans population were vulnerable not because of geography but because of long term class and race abandonment—poverty—exacerbated by the dismantling of social welfare by Democratic and Republican administrations alike; the incompetence of FEMA preparations expressed cocooned ruling class comradery, cronyism and privilege rather than any concern for the poor and working class; and the reconstruction looks set to capitalize on these inequalities and deepen them further. Not at any point in the next few decades will African Americans again account for two-thirds of New Orleans' population.

Government Intervention Can Help Prevent Disaster

There are alternatives. The Kyoto protocols [international agreement to limit greenhouse emmissions] were far from perfect but they represented a lowest common denominator in fighting global warming that the US would not even sign onto. As regards preparedness, both Oxfam America and the United Nations [UN] have pointed to Cuba as a plausible model. When Hurricane Ivan stormed through the Caribbean in September 2004, 27 people died in Florida and almost 100 in Granada, yet none died in Cuba which also took a direct hit on its west end. They were not always so successful, but the UN and Oxfam credit their record to several factors. First, Cubans learn from an early age about the danger of hurricanes and how to prepare and respond. Second, before the hurricane hits, local communities organize cleanup to secure potentially dangerous debris. Third, preparation and evacuation are organized and coordinated between the central government and local communities, and transportation away from danger is organized as a social community project rather than left to the private market, as happened in New Orleans and Houston. To prevent fires, gas and electricity supplies are cut off before the hurricane hits. During a hurricane, pre-organized state-sponsored emergency teams guarantee water, food and medical treatment—2,000 such teams in the case of Ivan. The government also organizes resources for communities to reconstruct.

By contrast, post-Katrina reconstruction in the United States will be dominated by top-down government contracts for tens if not hundreds of billions of dollars to major corporations and by billions of dollars of insurance payments to property owners so that they can reconstruct in the same vulnerable locations already destroyed. Such a solution may be good if measured by the yardstick of capitalist profit—a new buying binge by the Gulf raises all yachts, and, incredibly, insurance company stocks tend to rise following major disasters—but the same private market logic that caused such social destruction spells social and environmental disaster for those not in line to profit from government contracts and property insurance payments.

But there is an alternative. "We will not stand idly by while this disaster is used as an opportunity to replace our homes with newly built mansions and condos in a gentrified New Orleans," reads a statement from a citywide coalition of New Orleans low-income groups, Community Labor United. They went on to insist that the rebuilding of the city not be dominated by top-down corporate welfare but that those evacuated from New Orleans have the primary power over how the reconstruction proceeds. The billions of dollars already committed by Congress and the funds raised by charities belong by rights to the victims. Some will respond that reconstruction is very complicated, and it is, but the record of companies like Bechtel and Haliburton in Iraq are hardly evidence for the defense of a top-down Iraq model for New Orleans.

In the end, the reconstruction question is only secondarily technical. It is in the first place political, and the same corporate and federal abandonment that fostered such a widespread disaster can hardly be expected to perform an about-turn by empowering a disempowered population. Given the visceral response to the hundreds of unnecessary deaths resulting from Katrina, any attempt to impose a top-down solution by force is likely to incite an equally visceral response from below. If the Bush administration's first instinct was to eschew government and trust private charities to help the victims of Katrina, it should follow that instinct as regards the ordinary refugees of New Orleans and their ability to rebuild from the bottom up. There is no such thing as a natural disaster, and the supposed naturalness of the market is the last place to look for a solution to this disastrous havoc.

10

Disasters Increase with Misguided Socio-Economic Change

Daniel Sarewitz and Roger Pielke Jr.

Daniel Sarewitz is the director of the Consortium for Science, Policy, and Outcomes. His most recent book is Living with the Genie: Essays on Technology and the Quest for Human Mastery *(co-edited with Alan Lightman and Christina Desser). Roger Pielke Jr. is a professor in the environmental studies program at the University of Colorado and a fellow of the Cooperative Institute for Research in Environmental Sciences (CIRES).*

Global climate change is real, but reducing greenhouse gas emissions is not the answer to the threat of natural disasters. Instead, communities need to be prepared in order to face storms, droughts, or earthquakes. Most population growth occurs in cities on coastal or flood plains, or in earthquake zones, and most often the poor population is disproportionately affected. Causes for the recent disasters are socioeconomic change, and unless disaster preparedness is stressed alongside—but separate from—reducing emissions, many more lives will be claimed by catastrophes.

The increasing threat of natural disasters has long been cited as one of many reasons why society should reduce greenhouse gas emissions, and the horrendous toll of the December 26 [2004] Indonesian earthquake and resulting tsu-

Daniel Sarewitz and Roger Pielke, Jr., "Rising Tide: The Tsunami's Real Cause," The New Republic Online, January 17, 2005. Reproduced by permission of *The New Republic*.

nami has only made those calls louder. A December 30 article in *Salon* portrays the effects of the recent tsunami as "visions of just the kind of tumultuous weather that scientists have long viewed as a symptom of global warming." A day later, Sir David King, Britain's chief science adviser, told the BBC, "What is happening in the Indian Ocean underlines the importance of the Earth's system to our ability to live safely. And what we are talking about in terms of climate change is something that is really driven by our own use of fossil fuels."

Such arguments have a rich pedigree. Only nine days before the tsunami, Klaus Toepfer, executive director of the U.N. [United Nations] Environment Programme, said, "Climate scientists anticipate an increase [in] intensity of extreme weather events." Environmental groups use the threat of increasing disasters to advocate decisive action to reduce the emission of greenhouse gases and implement the Kyoto Protocol on climate change. The advocacy group Scientists and Engineers for Change supported [presidential candidate] John Kerry in the 2004 election by posting billboards in storm-ravaged Florida with the message, *Global Warming = Worse Hurricanes. George Bush just doesn't get it.*

Global climate change is real, and developing alternative energy sources and reducing global carbon-dioxide emission is essential.

Global climate change is real, and developing alternative energy sources and reducing global carbon-dioxide emission is essential. But the claim that action to slow climate change is justified by the rising toll of natural disasters—and, by extension, that reducing emissions can help stanch these rising losses—is both scientifically and morally insupportable. To minimize damage from tsunamis and the like, we need to focus not on reducing emissions but on reducing our vulnerability to disasters.

Disasters Are on the Rise

The first thing to understand about disasters is that they have indeed been rapidly increasing worldwide over the past century, in both number and severity, and that the causes of this increase are well understood—and have nothing to do with global warming. Data from the Center for Research on the Epidemiology of Disasters in Brussels, Belgium, as well as the Red Cross and the reinsurance industry, show that the number of disasters affecting at least 100 people or resulting in a call for international assistance has increased from an average of about 100 per year in the late '60s to between 500 and 800 per year by the early twenty-first century. The reason is not an increase in the frequency or severity of storms, earthquakes, or similar events, but an increase in vulnerability because of growing populations, expanding economies, rapid urbanization, and migrations to coasts and other exposed regions.

These changes are reflected in the costs of major disasters, which, according to the German insurance company Munich Re, rose more than tenfold in the second half of the twentieth century, from an average of about $4 billion per year in the 1950s to more than $40 billion in the 1990s, in inflation-adjusted dollars. The great Miami hurricane of 1926, for example, caused about $76 million in damage; when Hurricane Andrew, of similar force, struck South Florida in 1992, it caused more than $30 billion in damage, again adjusted for inflation. Research suggests that, if the same 1926 storm were to hit Miami today, it would cost more than $80 billion.

Poor Countries Suffer Exponentially

The economic losses from disasters are increasingly concentrated in the affluent world. But, as a percentage of GNP [gross national product], the economic effects of natural disasters on poor countries can be hundreds of times greater. Damages from Hurricane Mitch, for example, which devastated Central America in 1998, were estimated at between $5 and $7 billion—or almost the annual combined total economic activity of the two hardest-hit nations, Honduras and Nicaragua. Their economies still have not recovered. By comparison, the magnitude 6.7 earthquake that struck California in 1994, one of the costliest disasters in U.S. history, caused an estimated $20 to $40 billion in losses, but this amounted to only 2 to 4 percent of California's economic activity.

Emergency preparation and response capabilities are often inadequate, and hazard insurance is usually unavailable, further slowing recovery.

Disasters disproportionately harm poor people in poor countries because those countries typically have densely populated coastal regions, shoddily constructed buildings, sparse infrastructure, and grossly inadequate public health capabilities. Poor land use leads to widespread environmental degradation, such as deforestation and wetlands destruction, which in turn exacerbates flooding and landslides. Emergency preparation and response capabilities are often inadequate, and hazard insurance is usually unavailable, further slowing recovery. Thus, while the world's poorest 35 countries make up only about 10 percent of the world's population, they suffered more than half of the disaster-related deaths between 1992 and 2001.

Disparities in disaster vulnerability between rich and poor will continue to grow. About 97 percent of population growth is occurring in the developing world. This growth, in turn, drives urbanization and coastal migration. The result is that, in the next two decades, the population of urban areas in the developing world will likely increase by two billion people. And this population is being added to cities that are mostly located on coastal or flood plains—or in earthquake zones— and are unable to provide the quality of housing, services, infrastructure, and environmental protection that can help reduce vulnerability. Uncontrolled urban growth exacerbates hazards and urban growth.

Greenhouse Gas Emissions Are Not the Culprit

Faced with the inescapable momentum of these socioeconomic trends as we clean up from the South Asian disaster, the crucial question is this: What can be done to better prepare the world—especially the developing world—for future disasters? It is absurd to suggest that reducing greenhouse gas emissions is an important part of the answer.

The world will indeed be more vulnerable to tsunamis in the future, but, once again, the causes are primarily socioeconomic change, not climate change.

The chief reason is that the role of demographics in making a country vulnerable to disaster overwhelms that of a warming atmosphere. Indeed, the most recent assessment of the scientifically authoritative Intergovernmental Panel on Climate Change (IPCC) found no evidence to support the idea that human-caused climate change has discernibly influenced the rapidly increasing disaster toll of recent decades. While IPCC data and predictions indicate that human-caused climate change may have an effect on future disasters, our analysis of hurricanes and tropical cyclones, using IPCC data and assumptions, shows that, for every $1 of additional disaster damage scientists expect will be caused by the effects of global warming by 2050, an additional $22 to $60 of damages will result from the growth of economies and populations. Other studies of hurricanes, flooding, and heat waves lead to a similar conclusion: Socioeconomic trends, not climate change, will continue to drive increasing disaster losses.

The example of rising sea levels provides further illustration. Scientists expect that, by 2050, average global sea levels will rise by two to twelve inches. But no research suggests that the Kyoto Protocol, or even more ambitious emissions-reduction proposals, would significantly reduce this increase. Meanwhile, coastal populations will continue to grow by hundreds of millions, mostly in developing countries. Bangladesh alone, which suffered about 140,000 deaths from a cyclone in 1991, may add up to 100 million people to its population by 2050. The world will indeed be more vulnerable to tsunamis in the future, but, once again, the causes are primarily socio-economic change, not climate change.

Yet assertions that global warming is directly linked to rising disaster losses persist. Such assertions may have short-term political benefits in the global warming debate, but they detract from serious efforts to prepare for disasters. Global climate change has been a potent focusing lens for environmental groups, governments, the scientific research establishment, and international bodies, especially the United Nations [U.N.]. The U.N. Framework Convention on Climate Change—and its Kyoto Protocol mandating emissions reductions—occupies thousands of advocates, diplomats, scientists, lawyers, and journalists. The climate change policy agenda has also sucked into its maw a wide range of other issues, such as energy policy, water policy, public health and infectious diseases, deforestation, and, of course, disasters. Climate change thus captures a huge proportion of the public attention, political energy, and financial and intellectual resources available for addressing global environmental challenges—including disaster preparedness.

Disaster Research Is Underfunded

The U.N. Framework Convention, for example, refused to fund disaster preparedness efforts at its last conference in December [2004] unless states could demonstrate exactly how the disasters they feared were linked to climate change. Consider, too, the amount spent on scientific research. According to a recent RAND [Corporation] study, U.S. funding of disaster loss-reduction research in 2003 amounted to about $127 million—only 7 percent of the amount invested in climate change research for that year. Efforts in Congress to create a coordinated research program focused on reducing disaster losses have never gained momentum. By contrast, the U.S. government has sponsored a coordinated, multi-agency framework for climate change research for more than 15 years, with total investments, by our calculations, of more than $30 billion, adjusted for inflation.

This is not to say that many thousands of people and hundreds of organizations worldwide are not productively confronting disaster vulnerability, but their efforts do not begin to address the magnitude of the problem. Thousands of participants from most of the world's nations, along with scientists and political advocates, have come together every year since 1995 to work toward concerted international action on climate change. But, when the U.N. World Conference on Disaster Reduction convenes later this week [January 2005], it will be the first such meeting in more than a decade.

While the prospects for global climate change are constantly in the public eye, the South Asian earthquake and tsunami poignantly demonstrate that the crisis of growing disaster vulnerability only becomes news after disaster strikes. Yet we know that effective action is possible to reduce disaster losses even in the face of poverty and dense population. During the 2004 hurricane season, Haiti and the Dominican Republic, both on the island of Hispaniola, provided a powerful lesson in this regard. As Julia Taft of the U.N. Development Program explained: "In the Dominican Republic, which has invested in hurricane shelters and emergency evacuation networks, the death toll was fewer than ten, as compared to an estimated two thousand in Haiti. . . . Haitians were a hundred times more likely to die in an equivalent storm than Dominicans."

The question is why disaster vulnerability is so low on the list of global development priorities.

Most tools needed to reduce disaster vulnerability already exist, such as risk assessment techniques, better building codes and code enforcement, land-use standards, and emergency-preparedness plans. The question is why disaster vulnerability is so low on the list of global development priorities. Says Brian Tucker, president of GeoHazards International, "The most serious flaw in our current efforts is the lack of a globally accepted standard of acceptable disaster vulnerability, and an action plan to put every country on course to achieve this standard. Then we would have a means to measure progress and to make it clear which countries are doing well and which are not. We need a natural disaster equivalent to the Kyoto Protocol."

Toward a More Honest Discourse

Those who justify the need for greenhouse gas reductions by exploiting the mounting human and economic toll of natural disasters worldwide are either ill-informed or dishonest. This is not, as Britain's Sir David King suggested, "something we can manage" by decreasing our use of fossil fuels. Prescribing emissions reductions to forestall the future effects of disasters is like telling someone who is sedentary, obese, and alcoholic that the best way to improve his health is to wear a seat belt.

In principle, fruitful action on both climate change and disasters should proceed simultaneously. In practice, this will not happen until the issues of climate change and disaster vulnerability are clearly separated in the eyes of the media, the public, environmental activists, scientists, and policymakers.

As long as people think that *Global Warming* = *Worse Hurricanes*, global warming will also equal less preparation. And disasters will claim ever more money and lives.

11

U.S. Natural Disasters Are Becoming Ever More Costly

Gregory van der Vink et. al.

Gregory van der Vink is a visiting lecturer in geosciences at Princeton University. His area of specialization is on predicting potential human responses to environmental change that impact poverty-reduction efforts and that are precursors for conflict.

The federal government continues to provide disaster relief, even though the costs have vastly increased. In order to handle future natural disasters properly, it is of the essence that developments in high risk areas are discouraged, and that communities prepare more effectively for possible events. But even precautions are dangerous, if they encourage more people to settle in high-risk areas. If disaster relief effort and redevelopment are undertaken without changing the make-up of communities and their disaster preparedness, the costs of disasters will continue to rise.

The U.S. government, as the insurer of last resort, is becoming increasingly vulnerable to the costs of natural disasters through disaster declarations and spending by the Federal Emergency Management Agency (FEMA). The number of presidential disaster declarations has generally increased over the last half century, since the federal government has assumed continuous responsibility for disaster aid. The federal government's costs for natural disasters are increasing both in terms of the federal budget and the gross domestic product (GDP).

Gregory van der Vink et. al., "The Increasing Costs of U.S. Natural Disasters," *Geotimes*, November 2005. Reproduced by permission.

Even when accounting for the exponential rise in GDP over the last four decades, costs of natural disasters as a percentage of GDP have more than tripled. This figure does not include the recent costs from Hurricane Katrina [August 2005], which will most likely be the most expensive disaster in U.S. history, and has raised fundamental questions about high-risk land use.

Even when accounting for the exponential rise in GDP over the last four decades, costs of natural disasters as a percentage of GDP have more than tripled.

Rising Costs of Relief Efforts

The costs of natural disasters are driven by relatively few events—fewer than 1 percent of disaster declarations are responsible for the majority of costs. To reduce our nation's exposure to natural disasters, we need to determine what factors cause these few events to be so expensive.

In general, the increase in cost correlates strongly with the large increases in population and wealth in disaster-prone areas—in particular, East Coast regions vulnerable to hurricanes and West Coast regions vulnerable to earthquakes. By directly comparing disaster costs with local infrastructure costs, event size and event frequency, however, more subtle relationships emerge. Earthquakes, hurricanes, tornadoes and floods vary in frequency and impact, but all have the capability of inflicting great damage and incurring high costs to the federal government. U.S. hazard mitigation efforts and disaster relief policies may inadvertently be contributing to these increased costs by making us more vulnerable to expensive low-probability, high-cost events. The political and social forces that support these counterproductive policies will require a national change in how we perceive these disasters—a change that hurricanes Katrina and Rita may help initiate.

Hurricanes Are Complex and Unpredictable On the Move

In the last century, more than 170 hurricanes have hit the United States [as of 2005]. Each year in the Atlantic, approximately six hurricanes form, with one or two making landfall on the United States. Hurricane frequency, strength and location are affected by wind shear and sea-surface temperatures, both of which are part of the greater El Niño-Southern Oscillation and multi-decadal cycles and patterns.

Despite this year's highly active Atlantic hurricane season, there does not appear to have been a significant increase in either the occurrence or the severity of hurricanes over the last century; El Niño and La Niña provide an explanation for which years have more or fewer. During an El Niño phase, the sea surface temperature anomaly in the Pacific Ocean is high, and the number of storms in the Atlantic is low (in 1983 for example). During La Niña (the opposite of El Niño), the anomaly is low and the number of storms is high (in 1988 for example).

Hurricanes are complex events, having a diverse set of factors that drives damages in the areas they strike. Wind speeds, intense rainfall, coastal storm surges, unpredictable paths and varying travel speeds are among the characteristics that, together, define each hurricane event. In general, the physical and temporal uniqueness of each hurricane event mean that a large portion of the cost is the result of coincidental damages. Katrina, for example, would not have generated so much flooding if it had not moved so slowly over the coastal areas it affected.

The quantifiable storm characteristic that is most strongly correlated with FEMA spending is population density in the county where landfall occurred for large events, of Category 3 or higher on the Safir-Simpson scale.

Hurricanes typically strike coastal areas with strength, but weaken quickly after making landfall. Coastal areas, already at risk of storm-surge flooding, are therefore subject to more forceful winds. Increases in sea level, the inevitable landward migration of East Coast barrier islands and the continued population shift to coastal areas on the East Coast—which includes building high-value beachfront property—result in higher damage costs from hurricanes that make landfall, though the number of storms has not been increasing.

The more typical and less severe Category-1 or 2 events, which are not hugely different from a harsh rainstorm, show little or no correlation between FEMA spending and population density at landfall. The more forceful (and rare) events, as with earthquakes above magnitude 6.0, show a strong correlation between FEMA spending and population density.

Earthquake Damage Depends on Population Density

Between 1989 and 2004, more than 180 earthquakes of magnitude 5 or greater have struck in the continental United States. U.S. presidents have declared 11 of these events disasters.

As with hurricanes, earthquake costs are determined by the population impacted. The relationship between cost and population becomes apparent by comparing earthquake size and population density between 1989 and 2004. When FEMA awarded money to an area with a moderate or high population density (200 to 1,800 people per square mile) affected by an earthquake of a magnitude greater than 6.5, the funding increased with the population density irrespective of the magnitude of the event (for example, the Northridge [Calif.], Loma Prieta [Calif.] and Olympia [Wash.] quakes). When FEMA awarded money to an earthquake-affected area with low population density (20 to 200 people per square mile), the funding scaled with the magnitude of the event (for example, the Landers [Calif.], Petrolia [Calif.], San Simeon [Calif.], Clackamas [Ore.], Napa [Calif.] and Plattsburgh [N.Y.]

quakes). When FEMA awarded money to an earthquake-affected area with a very low population density (between 0 and 20 people per square mile), the funding was small—approximately $5 million—irrespective of the magnitude of the event (such as with the Denali [Alaska] and Klamath [Ore.] quakes).

Tornadoes Show No Real Increase in Frequency or Cost

Between 1989 and 2004, 155 disaster declarations have included the word "tornado" in their description. The size of tornadoes is described by the Fujita scale F0 to F5 (similar to the magnitude of an earthquake or the category of a hurricane). A dramatic increase in reported F0 events occurred in the late 1980s, due to the introduction of Doppler 88-D surveillance radar; more events were detected and therefore more reported. After removing the F0 events, the frequency of tornadoes over the last 20 years shows no increase.

More than 85 percent of U.S. counties have been declared federal disaster areas due to floods in the past 50 years.

Most tornadoes occur in the central United States, where population densities are low (between 20 and 200 people per square mile) and relatively uniform. Tornadoes are also short-lived and affect only small areas. For a tornado to incur a high cost, it must occur along with significant flooding, or be a unique event in terms of what it destroys. On March 14, 1997, for example, an F5 tornado destroyed an airplane hangar in Kentucky containing expensive aircraft, and in another case, on May 4, 1999, an F5 event included a cluster of 94 tornadoes occurring over two days in the Oklahoma City region.

In contrast to earthquakes and hurricanes, which are low-frequency, high-cost events, tornadoes exemplify high-frequency, low-cost events. Tornado events are similar in cost—typically less than $25 million—because they occur frequently in areas of moderate to low population density.

Floods Necessitate Anticipation and Preparation

Because of the complex nature of rivers and their drainage basins, defining one standard that successfully measures a flood is difficult. No scale exists for floods that is similar to the magnitude scale for earthquakes, the Fujita scale for tornadoes or the category system for hurricanes. Recurrence intervals are used to measure the size of a flood, but the measurements are unique to a drainage basin and do not allow comparisons among different drainage basins.

More than 85 percent of U.S. counties have been declared federal disaster areas due to floods in the past 50 years. With increasing development in floodplains, less soil is available to soak up water, and flooding occurs more easily than ever. Floods are such high-frequency, ubiquitous events that much has already been done to ameliorate effects of common flooding disasters. On a local scale, the cost-effectiveness of further flood control measures is questionable, especially in areas not normally prone to flooding. On a national scale, however, floods constitute a high portion of FEMA's disaster obligations.

The 20 most expensive floods in the United States show that costs roughly depend on population density. However, five of these 20 floods do not follow this trend. These outlying events are either extremely large, such as the Mississippi River flood in 1993, or occurred in areas unprepared for a flood, such as Detroit, Mich., in 2000. As with tornadoes, the relationship suggests that the driving factor of the cost of expensive floods is the unusual nature of the event with regard to its magnitude or its location.

Politics Don't Often Influence Relief for the Better

For extreme events, disasters can also be a test of governments, as the world has witnessed with Hurricane Katrina. Disasters can bond a community and provide opportunities for politicians to demonstrate leadership. In fact, political support for incumbent politicians commonly increases following a disaster. Conversely, if a government fails to respond properly, disasters can also foment political unrest. On a small scale, they can change public opinion of a leader, as illustrated by polls that showed lower approval ratings of President [George W.] Bush following Katrina. And on the larger scale, they can even result in the overthrow of governments, as in the case of the 1972 Managua earthquake, when the vast destruction contributed to the unrest that eventually led the Nicaraguan people to oust General Somoza.

In the United States, usually the governor of the affected state makes a formal request for FEMA assistance. Because a presidential disaster declaration is required before FEMA can provide an area with federal disaster relief funding, political factors can be introduced into the process. Based on records from 1952 to 2002, whether the U.S. president and the state governor shared a party affiliation had no significant effect on whether a disaster declaration would be approved or turned down. Furthermore, Republican and Democratic administrations have similar approval and denial rates.

Although party politics do not seem to play a major role in disaster funding, almost every election year shows a small spike in the number of disaster relief requests approved—particularly when the incumbent is running for reelection. Meeting symbolically with disaster victims and approving requests for disaster funding are attractive opportunities for a candidate to improve his or her public image. The minor year-to-year political fluctuations are small, however, when viewed in the context of the overall increase in disaster declarations with time.

Opportunity for Change

The timescale of human experience is short compared to the recurrence interval of many natural phenomena. While we develop infrastructure resilient to common events, such as routine seasonal weather, we remain vulnerable to those events that occur less frequently or over longer timescales. For example, a 6-inch snowfall in Boston, where such storms occur annually, has much less impact than a 6-inch snowfall in Washington, D.C., where such storms occur only once a decade.

We tend to view natural disasters as random unfortunate acts, rather than the predictable consequence of high-risk land use.

When considering events that garner a FEMA disaster declaration, two cost-frequency trends emerge. Earthquake and hurricane disasters are generally high-cost, low-frequency events, whereas tornado and flood disasters are low-cost, high-frequency events. The common factor for high cost is the extent to which the disaster is unusual—either in terms of its recurrence interval or its size. In other words, rare events such as earthquakes and hurricanes just need to happen in populated areas to be costly. More frequent events, such as tornadoes and floods, need to be unusually large or to occur in areas where they usually do not occur.

In the United States, the increase in costs to the federal government is most likely an unforeseen consequence of our own disaster management policies. Mitigation strategies require public support; public support requires awareness; and awareness usually requires the occurrence of an event. As a result, resources are almost always available to respond to the last event, but rarely to mitigate against the next. We tend to view natural disasters as random unfortunate acts, rather than the predictable consequence of high-risk land use. As a result, we rebuild communities in the same high-risk areas—thus inadvertently using taxpayer dollars to put more people in harm's way.

In many cases, the influx of federal assistance and rebuilding can actually boost the local economy—resulting in more infrastructure and increased population in these high-risk areas. Such efforts may, themselves, then become responsible for increased costs. Whether it is cost-effective for communities to maintain a state of readiness for low-probability events, such as a "storm of the century" or even a "storm of the decade," is questionable.

Precautions Breed Disaster

Mitigation against moderate events can make us more vulnerable to large events. For example, a levee may be enlarged to handle a 100-year storm rather than a 50-year storm. If the net result of the rebuilding is four times as many people move into the area, the risk ends up increasing. Paradoxically, our mitigation efforts, like our response efforts, subsidize such high-risk land use as living on migrating barrier islands, in floodplains or on active fault zones.

Consequently, we are becoming more vulnerable to low-probability events. For any specific individual city, this short-term solution is politically and, with federal disaster relief, economically attractive. When such an approach is adopted across a nation, however, the result increases already large costs to the federal government.

Population trends, mitigation efforts and federal disaster relief policies all contribute to encouraging high-risk land use and ultimately to making our society more vulnerable to the costs of natural disasters. Hurricane Katrina has created an opportunity to change this trend at the national scale. If New Orleans is built to accommodate the inevitable next extreme hurricane, it will set an example for future land-use management and urban planning. Absent such change, the costs of natural disasters, and the government's liability, will simply continue to increase as we place more people and infrastructure in harm's way.

12

Natural Disasters Can Boost Economies

Drake Bennett

Drake Bennett is a writer for The Boston Globe.

Studies seem to indicate that areas affected by natural disasters improved their infrastructure in the course of redevelopment and boosted their economy for years to come. Yet research on the positive economic effects of disasters is met with hate and skepticism, because the data are open for interpretation and the measuring tools are not exact enough. Furthermore, economic growth after disasters appears to benefit exclusively the wealthy and drive less affluent inhabitants from their homes and neighborhoods. Yet applying post-disaster urgency to general development might boost economies without the bitter taste of disaster.

The earthquake that struck China's Sichuan Province in May [2008] left behind scenes of almost apocalyptic devastation: mountaintops sheared off into valleys, cities reduced to rubble and dust, cracked dams, collapsed bridges, and at least 80,000 dead.

If the Chinese government is to be believed, the earthquake also did something else: it helped the country's economy. A little over a month after the quake, the State Information Center, a Chinese government research body, announced that the massive rebuilding effort, and the billions of dollars it would pump into the Chinese economy, would far

Drake Bennett, "How Disasters Help," *The Boston Globe*, July 6, 2008. Reproduced by permission.

outweigh the economic losses from the quake, enough to bump up national economic growth by 0.3 percent—a small but not insignificant part of a 2008 growth rate most estimates put at just under 10 percent.

Disasters Stimulate Economic Growth

Traditionally, analysts have cautioned that Chinese growth figures should be greeted with skepticism, but, according to one school of economic thought, there may be something to the idea that the quake served as a brutal stimulus. In fact, some economists argue that hurricanes, earthquakes, floods, volcanic eruptions, ice storms, and the like, despite the widespread destruction they leave behind—indeed, largely because of it—can spur economic growth.

Some of the most recent work has found a link between disasters and subsequent innovation.

Rebuilding efforts serve as a short-term boost by attracting resources to a country, and the disasters themselves, by destroying old factories and old roads, airports, and bridges, allow new and more efficient public and private infrastructure to be built, forcing the transition to a sleeker, more productive economy in the long term.

"When something is destroyed you don't necessarily rebuild the same thing that you had. You might use updated technology, you might do things more efficiently. It bumps you up," says Mark Skidmore, an economics professor at Michigan State University. "Disasters help people think about things differently."

Studies have found that earthquakes in California and Alaska helped stir economic activity there, and that countries with more hurricanes and storms tend to see higher rates of growth. Some of the most recent work has found a link between disasters and subsequent innovation.

The study of the economics of disasters remains a small field, with few major papers. And skeptics charge disaster economists with oversimplifying enormously complex economic systems and seeing illusory effects that stem only from the crudeness of the available economic measuring tools.

Disaster Research Can Also Boost Low-Risk Communities

But as more people move to riskier areas, and the world's climate shifts, the debate over natural disasters and their impact has been gaining in resonance. The population of coastal hurricane zones and cities, from San Francisco to Mexico City to Tokyo, that sit on or near major seismic faults, continues to grow, and climatologists warn that climate change could increase the number of extreme weather events in many parts of the world. While not even the most fervent believer in the economy-catalyzing qualities of disasters would wish for one, the study of the costs and possible benefits of such events may help us better understand how to target recovery efforts—and, perhaps, how to replicate the salutary effects of disasters without the disasters themselves.

The economic study of natural disasters has roots in the study of human disasters—in particular, the effects of wars, real and imagined. In the 1950s and 1960s, analysts at the RAND Corporation think tank, trying to work out the total impact of a nuclear attack on the United States, created models for how such an attack would affect our economy. The best-known of these thinkers was Herman Kahn, a physicist and systems analyst notorious for his willingness, even eagerness, to reduce the seemingly unthinkable to dry actuarial calculations. In his 1961 book, *On Thermonuclear War*, Kahn wrote that, thanks to the United States' strong growth rate at the time, even a nuclear attack that destroyed all of its major metropolitan areas and killed one-third of its population "does not seem to be a total economic catastrophe. It may simply set the nation's productive capacity back a decade or two plus destroying many 'luxuries.'"

Natural disasters provided an opportunity to see how societies actually recovered from such large-scale shocks. In 1969, Douglas Dacy and Howard Kunreuther, two young analysts at the Institute for Defense Analyses, published a book called *The Economics of Natural Disasters*, one of the first attempts to quantify the economic impact of catastrophes. The book was largely a case study of the Great Alaska Earthquake of 1964, the most powerful ever recorded in North America. Dacy and Kunreuther found that the money that rushed into the Alaskan economy after the temblor, as well as generous government loans and grants for rebuilding, meant that many Alaskans were actually better off afterward than before.

Unpopular Research

"We got a lot of hate mail for that finding," recalls Kunreuther, now a professor of business and public policy at the University of Pennsylvania's Wharton School.

But though it may have proved unpopular among Alaskans still dealing with the aftermath of the disaster—which killed 131 people, destroyed several towns along the Alaskan coast, and leveled portions of Anchorage—the idea that disasters trigger short-term growth has gained adherents among economists.

"The data are pretty clear about it," says Gus Faucher, director of macroeconomics at Moody's *Economy.com*, an economic consulting firm.

Faucher has looked at disasters in regional US economies and found in some cases a dramatic impact. The year after Hurricane Andrew struck southeast Florida in 1992, causing what would today be more than $40 billion in damages, the state saw sharp increases in employment thanks to new construction jobs. And Faucher credits the rebuilding jobs and aid and investment that followed the 1994 Northridge earthquake for helping pull the Los Angeles area out of its early-1990s economic slump. Hurricane Katrina [2005], Faucher says, has proved an exception: Because so many residents left the area and because government aid was so slow to arrive and insurance payouts so low, the area didn't see an economic bounce.

To critics of this line of thinking, the problem is that it is, at best, a partial picture. It ignores, they argue, the fact that the money and labor that go into post-disaster rebuilding are simply being redirected from other productive uses.

"If you're a carpenter, a trash remover, a physician, you may be made better off, but the things that those producers would have otherwise produced are not going to be produced," says Donald Boudreaux, an economics professor at George Mason University. "Over any reasonably relevant period of time, society is not made wealthier by destroying resources," he adds. If it were, "Beirut should be one of the wealthiest places in the world."

The economy, as it recovers, actually becomes more productive than it was before, and some economists argue that the effect can be seen decades after the disaster.

Weeding Out Old Infrastructure

The research on longer-run effects, its supporters argue, is less vulnerable to this criticism, because the key factor is not merely new stuff but better stuff. In this model, disasters perform the economic service of clearing out outdated infrastructure to make way for more efficient replacements—Mother Nature's contribution to what the Austrian economist Joseph Schumpeter famously called capitalism's "creative destruction." The economy, as it recovers, actually becomes more productive than it was before, and some economists argue that the effect can be seen decades after the disaster.

When Dacy and Kunreuther looked at Alaska after the quake, they found that the state's fishing fleet, refurbished after being decimated by the ensuing tsunami, was able to increase its yield over pre-quake levels. And the building industry grew more innovative, as well. Whereas before, construction had been limited to the warmer months of the year, the pressure to rebuild quickly drove the adoption of new methods and technologies like the use of "visqueen" plastic films to protect construction sites, allowing work to continue year-round despite the bitter Alaskan winter.

Other, more recent academic work has taken a broader look at the question. Mark Skidmore of Michigan State, along with the economist Hideki Toya of Japan's Nagoya City University, published a 2002 paper in the journal *Economic Inquiry* that mapped the disaster frequency of 89 countries against their economic growth over a 30-year period. The paper controlled for everything the authors could think of that might skew the findings—including country size (large countries would presumably experience more natural disasters), size of government, openness to trade, and distance from the equator.

Skidmore and Toya found that, in the case of climatic disasters—hurricanes and cyclones, as opposed to earthquakes and volcanic eruptions—the more the better: nations with more climatic disasters grew faster over the long run than the less disaster-prone. Why only climatic disasters? The authors suggest that, as we've gotten better at forecasting violent weather, its human costs, at least, can be mitigated much more easily than with geological disasters, which still take us by surprise.

Jesus Crespo Cuaresma, a professor of economics at the University of Innsbruck, has found some support for Skidmore and Toya's argument. In a paper published earlier this year [2008], Crespo Cuaresma examined post-disaster rebuilding efforts in developing countries and found that, at least in wealthier developing countries like Brazil and South Africa, there is indeed a tendency to use the rebuilding process as an opportunity to upgrade infrastructure that might otherwise have been allowed to grow obsolete.

Measuring Tools Are too Crude

Other work, however, has challenged the disaster-growth linkage. Ilan Noy, an assistant professor of economics at the University of Hawaii, has looked at long-term growth and disaster data and found that natural disasters hurt growth in the short term, and can barely be said to have any effect over the long run. According to Noy, the problem with studies that see a long-term positive effect is that their measurements are too crude—they average growth over decades rather than breaking it down into shorter periods of time, and they don't account for the varying severity of the disasters in question.

A recovery planned only to maximize growth might well conflict with more basic humanitarian concerns.

Like Crespo Cuaresma, Noy focused on developing countries (Noy argues that it would be impossible to find any impact at all on national economies in the wealthy world). And he concedes that aid money and materials do tend to stream in after a major catastrophe. It's just that at the same time an even greater amount of private money is leaving the country. "There's a perception that it's more of a dangerous place," he says.

Of course, even analysts of the "creative destruction" school don't see disasters as good things—disasters kill people, often in numbers, and uproot many more. Skidmore is careful to point out that, even from a coldly economic standpoint, the most productive disasters are those that don't take lives. In harming buildings but not people, they encourage societies to invest less in vulnerable, immovable things like factories, he argues, and more in human capital, in skills and education, "things that won't be destroyed if a disaster strikes," he says.

Only the Wealthy Win

Nonetheless, a recovery planned only to maximize growth might well conflict with more basic humanitarian concerns. Those most in need of help and resources in the wake of a disaster—the poor and the uninsured near-poor—are going to contribute the least to growing the economy as it recovers. On the other hand, those best equipped to find opportunities for growth in the rubble—large corporations and the wealthy—are also those best able to survive the catastrophe on their own.

"If you took all the disaster relief money and gave it out to the corporations affected, you will have spent a lot of money very intelligently in terms of urban growth," says Larry Rosenthal, executive director of the program on housing and urban policy at the University of California, Berkeley, "but not in terms of fairness."

Indeed, disaster recovery has attracted critics who see it as a predatory industry in disguise; in a book published last fall called *The Shock Doctrine: The Rise of Disaster Capitalism*, the journalist Naomi Klein argued that corporations, first-world governments, and aid organizations treat natural disasters as chances to open up new markets—with dismal results for the recovering nations themselves.

It may be, then, that disaster economics works best as a guide in those times when we don't have disasters to contend with. Investing in human capital, replacing outdated plants and infrastructure—the things that Kunreuther and Skidmore argue disasters drive us to do—are also, it turns out, good ideas even in the absence of a crippling catastrophe. If the disaster economists are right, calamities are simply pushing societies to make the sort of sound economic decisions that inertia or fear or bureaucratic sclerosis prevents them from otherwise making. Governments and businesses might do well to adopt some of the urgency and innovation of a post-disaster mind-set even in more clement times.

13

Geoengineering Might Be Necessary to Fight Disaster

Gregory Lamb

Gregory Lamb is a writer for the Christian Science Monitor.

While reviled by environmentalists, geoengineering might provide an alternative to reducing greenhouse gas emissions and pollution. Its implications and longterm consequences are yet unknown, but the ability to create trees that can absorb large amounts of carbon dioxide or to block the sun's harmful rays could prove indispensable. Since reducing pollution has yet to prove effective, geoengineering could have a more immediate impact.

Launch myriad mirrors into space to deflect a fraction of sunlight from reaching Earth. Seed the stratosphere with sulfur or other particles to cut some of the sun's rays. Bioengineer trees to soak up huge amounts of carbon dioxide from the air. Scatter unmanned self-powered ships to roam the world's oceans funneling sea spray high in the sky to help form protective clouds.

Thinkers have posed a number of creative ideas on how to protect the planet from global warming. But they've been dismissed by most environmentalists and many in the scientific community as science-fiction whimsy, at best. At worst, critics say, these schemes might have unexpected and potentially disastrous consequences or distract from the effort to cut greenhouse-gas emissions.

Gregory Lamb, "Can We Engineer a Cooler Earth?" *Christian Science Monitor*, July 16, 2008. Reproduced by permission from *Christian Science Monitor*. www.csmonitor.com.

But today, attitudes show signs of shifting as meaningful efforts by governments to cut emissions have proved elusive. More and more scientists and environmentalists despite their continuing reservations, are seeing "geoengineering" projects as a necessary backup plan. In June [2008], the top scientific academies in 13 countries, including the United States, joined in a call for more aggressive action against global warming, including serious consideration of geoengineering.

The Future Might Belong
to Geoengineering

At the same time, the Group of Eight leading economic powers meeting in Japan failed to set any near-term goals to reduce emissions. The group's soft, conditional goals for 2050 will be too little, too late, many environmentalists say.

"The reality is that de-carbonization is not happening fast enough," says Jamais Cascio, an environmentalist and futurist in northern California.

The need for geoengineering is "almost certain," he says.

The attitude among tech-friendly environmentalists, sometimes called "Bright Greens," has been shifting in favor of geoengineering, Mr. Cascio says. "This is by no means anyone's first choice, but it is better than the alternative," he says, which is unmitigated warming of the planet.

"I think that you'll see quite a few relatively desperate nation-states willing to try something like [geoengineering] simply to avoid global disaster," Cascio says. Since such efforts are very likely, in his view, the role of environmentalists will be to "make sure we do it in the way that is most responsible," he says.

Opponents remain unpersuaded and point to a litany of potential problems with geoengineering schemes. Chief among them is that efforts to engineer humanity's way out of the climate challenge are likely to distract from the hard work of mitigation: cutting greenhouse-gas emissions.

"To me, that [argument] doesn't make sense," says Samuel Thernstrom, a resident fellow studying public policy and geoengineering at the American Enterprise Institute (AEI) in Washington. No political leaders have said they would drop emission cuts in favor of geoengineering, nor do opinion polls indicate the public supports that idea, he says. In fact, Mr. Thernstrom argues, geoengineering is more likely to have the opposite effect. If a US president says we've got to start thinking about blocking the sun to cool the earth, "People are going to start taking mitigation [emission cuts] really seriously," he says.

Any scheme also could bring with it unintended consequences and hard-to-quantify costs.

Finding Common Ground Is Difficult

Geoengineering faces legal hurdles. Would nations or private enterprises undertake the projects? Would an international agreement need to be reached? Might countries work at cross purposes?

"What if India wanted it a couple of degrees colder, and Russia didn't mind it a couple of degrees warmer?" asks Alan Robock, an environmental sciences professor at Rutgers University in New Jersey. Last spring, Dr. Robock published a paper entitled "20 reasons why geoengineering may be a bad idea."

Such projects could also have military applications and as such could violate an existing global treaty that bans altering the climate for hostile purposes, he says. If the effects are salutary in one part of the world, but harmful in another, who decides what will be done? Any scheme also could bring with it unintended consequences and hard-to-quantify costs. Seeding the atmosphere with sulfur particles, for example, is likely to turn the sky whiter. "How do you quantify no more blue skies" as a cost, Robock asks. (One compensation: The number of fiery red and yellow sunsets would increase.)

A recent study using computer models showed that putting sun-deflecting mirrors in space would cool the Earth, but wouldn't return it to the way it was before human-generated global warming began.

"Some places get warmer, some places cool down ... some places get wetter, some places get drier," says lead author Dan Lunt, a climate modeler at Britain's University of Bristol. He calls the new climate that would emerge "Sunshade World," an Earth in which CO_2 [carbon dioxide] levels remain high but temperatures are moderated. The closest equivalent to that condition last occurred during the Cambrian period about 500 million years ago, the paper says.

The most talked about proposal would send sulfur or other fine particles high into earth's atmosphere using airplanes, balloons, or perhaps even artillery shells to block out a tiny fraction of the sunlight.

"The aerosol idea frightens people a lot," Thernstrom says. Sulfur is a pollutant, and studies show it would slightly increase acid rain over the poles. The polar ozone holes would close more slowly, with some ill effects. "But compared to the effects of uncontrolled warming, that's not that big a concern," he says.

Blocking sunlight, adds futurist Cascio, "is at best a delay of the worst temperature-related consequences of global warming in order to give us more time for de-carbonization."

Any long-term approach to solving global warming, Thernstrom says, almost certainly will have three aspects: emissions reductions, geoengineering, and steps to adapt to an altered climate. "The question is, 'What is the ratio among those three pieces?'"

Schemes to slightly dim sunlight also wouldn't solve the problem of ocean acidification, caused by airborne CO_2 entering seawater. More-acidic oceans would harm coral reefs and upset ocean ecology, with possible far-reaching effects. Ocean acidification is "at least as big" a problem as that of CO_2 in the air, Cascio says.

Geoengineering Might Be an Alternative to Mitigation

Despite the new buzz around geoengineering, including a recent seminar at AEI, some opponents are adamant. Raymond Pierrehumbert, a professor of geophysics at the University of Chicago, has proposed a 10-year moratorium on research into geoengineering, to ensure humanity isn't tempted to try this option.

But a new consensus seems to be forming around the idea of stepping up research, even as differences remain over when, if ever, to deploy such schemes. Robock, who maintains strong reservations, also favors research. "We have to know if it's reasonable or not, how long it might work, what the problems would be, how much it might cost," he says.

The US government now spends between $2 billion and $3 billion on global warming research, and will probably spend more under the next president. If just $100 million of that over five years were spent on geoengineering research, "We would learn an awful lot," Thernstrom says.

"The potential payoff is very large. If mitigation doesn't work, and we have every reason to believe it's not likely to [work] in the short term, . . . you kind of want to have a Plan B."

14

Earth's Biggest Catastrophe Might Still Be Ahead

Kirsten Weir

Kirsten Weir is a science writer.

Some scientists expect rising global temperatures to free up vast deposits of methane below the seafloor. Should that happen, temperatures would increase rapidly and dramatically, endangering life on Earth. Recently, expeditions have observed methane plumes in several areas of the Arctic Circle, and research is being conducted on how to use methane as an energy source. With or without methane though, the prospect of the atmosphere heating up remains scary.

By now we all know what's in store for us if we continue on our emissions-happy path: increasingly hotter days, horrific droughts and floods, angrier storms, acidic ocean waters that will dissolve coral reefs, and a surging sea level that will swallow our coastal cities. Still, that scenario is a virtual sunny day by the pool compared to the cataclysmic climate picture being drawn by some scientists. Never mind carbon dioxide emissions. Let's talk about the vast stores of carbon hidden deep beneath our feet.

During the last year [2008], geoscientists have held several workshops and conferences to discuss what is known—and the great deal that isn't—about the "deep carbon" cycle. Next week [December 2008], at the annual meeting of the Ameri-

Kirsten Weir, "Global Boiling," Salon.com, December 12, 2008. This article first appeared in Salon.com, at http://www.salon.com. An online version remains in the Salon archives. Reprinted with permission.

can Geophysical Union, scientists plan to hold a special session devoted to one potentially frightening aspect of that cycle: a strange little substance known as methane hydrate.

Temperatures Are Rising

Methane hydrates, or clathrates, are icelike gas deposits buried under permafrost and deep below the seafloor. Some researchers fear that the hydrates are on the verge of melting en masse and belching out a cloud of methane gas that will send global temperatures skyrocketing.

The doomsday scenario goes something like this: If global temperatures keep rising, some methane hydrates will melt, sending methane gas bubbling up through the ocean and into the atmosphere. Like any good greenhouse gas, the methane will trap heat close to Earth's surface, causing temperatures to climb even higher. Hotter temperatures will melt more hydrates, and on and on. In other words, methane hydrates could trigger the mother of all feedback loops. The story, says David Archer, a geophysicist at the University of Chicago, "has a great apocalyptic side to it."

Methane is the same natural gas that we burn for fuel. Under the right combination of intense pressures and chilly temperatures, the gas becomes trapped inside icy cages of hydrogen bonds. These methane hydrates look like chunks of ice, with the nifty difference that they eagerly burst into flame when sparked. Methane hydrates are also a lot less stable than your average ice cube. If the temperature rises or pressure eases, the hydrates essentially melt to form methane gas.

Methane hydrates aren't unusual, astronomically speaking. They exist on Mars, inside comets, and on at least a couple of Saturn's frosty moons. Here on Earth, they form deep below permafrost and under seafloor sediments, where temperature and pressure conspire to keep the structures stable. It's not certain how much methane is locked up in hydrates, but some estimates put the total as high as 10,000 gigatons, says Gerald

Dickens, a professor of earth sciences at Rice University. To put it in perspective, he says, "the estimates for all of the oil, gas, and coal [on Earth] is about 5,000 gigatons."

As a greenhouse gas, methane is in the big leagues, some 20 times as potent as carbon dioxide. If all the methane trapped underground were to wind up in the atmosphere, you could kiss your winter boots goodbye. "There is so much [methane hydrate] in the ocean that if you gave the planet a big shake and it came out all at once, it would be a climate disaster far worse than anything we have with carbon dioxide," Archer says.

Searching for Clues

Are we giving the planet that kind of shake? To predict the future, climate scientists begin by peering into the past. Human induced global warming may be a new trend, but Earth has certainly experienced rapid and dramatic climate changes in its ancient history. Methane hydrates may have played a role in a period of abrupt warming 635 million years ago, according to a paper published in *Nature* last spring. The researchers, from UC [University of California]-Riverside and Flinders University in Australia, point to high levels of methane present in the atmosphere at that time.

Around 55 million years ago, Earth again shifted abruptly from snowy to steamy. Many researchers have fingered hydrates in that warming spell, too. "Methane hydrates may not be the only explanation, but very likely played a large role," says Carolyn Ruppel, a research geophysicist with the U.S. Geological Survey, who will co-chair with Dickens the upcoming American Geophysical Union panel on hydrates.

James Kennett, a professor of earth sciences at UC-Santa Barbara, is a vocal proponent of the idea that methane hydrates have played a role in past climate changes. He also fears they are poised do so again. "The gas hydrates are inherently unstable with warming of the oceans. I can't see why [melting hydrates] would not be inevitable," he says. "The question is just how sensitive the system is."

Kennett argues that much of the geological research community has turned a blind eye to the evidence of methane hydrate's role in climate change. "It's a paradigm problem. The community is not prepared at this time to make a paradigm shift," he says. "[Climate change] is the biggest issue of our time. I think we need to look at this."

He suggests we start by taking a cold, hard look at the Arctic, where a great deal of methane hydrate exists in permafrost and under the continental shelf. Because of the extreme cold, hydrates are stable at shallower depths in the Arctic than anywhere else on Earth. Warm up the Arctic a bit, and these shallow hydrates will be the first to come apart, Kennett warns. "Is this already happening? Are we living in it now?"

Inside the Arctic Circle, the ocean is reportedly bubbling like a freshly uncorked magnum of Dom Perignon.

Methane Watch

Kennett has valid reasons for wondering. Inside the Arctic Circle, the ocean is reportedly bubbling like a freshly uncorked magnum of Dom Perignon [Champagne]. In September, scientists aboard a Russian research vessel described methane gas fizzing up from the seabed in several areas of the Arctic. Just a few days later, British scientists exploring the ocean west of the Norwegian island of Svalbard reported hundreds of these methane plumes.

It all sounds pretty ominous, but researchers aren't ready to attribute the recently observed methane bubbles in the Arctic to melting hydrates. Scientific reports of the plumes have not yet been published or peer-reviewed. Although Kennett is fearful of a methane catastrophe, he's not yet sure this is it. "I need to be convinced," he says.

He's not the only one. For one thing, says Archer, "there weren't observations before, so it's hard to say if it's a new phenomenon." Perhaps methane has been sputtering up from the Arctic for decades, with no one around to see it. What's more, many potential sources of methane exist. As bacteria break down thawing organic matter, they release the gas as a byproduct. "There's all this juicy organic carbon preserved in these areas," Archer points out. "These methane escapes could be from decomposing peat."

Ruppel, too, is a long way from ringing any alarm bells over the Arctic bubbles. "Perhaps people are jumping to conclusions before the story is really clear in the Arctic," she says. "My suspicion is that almost all of that methane has nothing to do with gas hydrates."

But let's imagine, for the sake of argument, that the Arctic gas plumes do turn out to be from methane hydrates. Does that mean it's curtains for life as we know it? Not necessarily.

"Methane beneath the permafrost is probably the most sensitive to change, but it's a small component of the total amount [of methane hydrates]," Dickens says. The vast majority is buried deep below the seafloor, he notes, and would be considerably harder to unlock. "At deep water depths, temperature would have to change 10 or 15 degrees Celsius to remove all the methane," Dickens estimates. "It would be very difficult for all of it to come out."

Low-Risk Methane

For that matter, adds Archer, it would be very difficult for even a portion of it to come out. "It would be arrogant to say it's impossible, but nobody has come up with a mechanism to get even 10 percent of this methane into the atmosphere," he says.

Even if methane hydrates did start melting, the gas would have to travel through hundreds of meters of mud and thousands of meters of water before it could mix with the air. "A lot of methane would dissolve in ocean waters," Ruppel says. "The ocean is very undersaturated with methane. It could accommodate a whole lot before the methane would get out into the atmosphere."

Furthermore, Dickens adds, it's not enough to show that methane can travel from the deep ocean to the atmosphere. One also has to consider the rate. "It is possible in the future that large amounts of methane can come out of these systems," he says. "Is it probable that significant amounts will come out in the next 100 years? Probably not."

Archer is also skeptical of the importance of methane hydrates in ancient global-warming events. "The evidence for these things being important for climate change in the past, I think, is kind of dodgy," he says. True, something released a lot of carbon into the atmosphere 55 million years ago. But maybe, he suggests, that something was a volcanic event that spewed methane gas, or a bunch of carbon-rich sediments that were suddenly lifted above sea level and exposed to the air. "There's no real clear smoking gun that it was methane hydrates," he says.

Ruppel says there's definitely more to learn. "I think the jury is still out on this," she says. But she doesn't see any reason for panic. The story that methane hydrates are a looming catastrophe "is a position some of us are working hard to counteract," she says.

Panic over methane hydrates is probably premature.

Becoming an Energy Source

In fact, much of the effort put into studying methane hydrates isn't focused on global warming at all, but on energy. The U.S. Department of Energy is taking a close look at mining methane hydrates for fuel, and they aren't the only ones. Countries including Japan, China and India are also exploring ways to turn hydrates into usable energy. "It is getting to the point now that methane hydrates could definitely become a viable commercial source for natural gas within the next 10 years," Ruppel says.

As a fuel, methane hydrate has some advantages. It's more accessible than conventional natural gas resources, Ruppel points out. And it is cleaner to burn and emits about half as much carbon dioxide as does coal. "Natural gas is probably the greenest of the fossil fuels," adds Archer.

But it is a fossil fuel, after all, and human-induced global warming is still a very real phenomenon. So will methane hydrates fuel our future, or destroy it? That may be the ultimate question, but not an easy one to resolve. For those willing to try, "it is a very interesting time in this field," Ruppel says. "We need more good science. I think we're moving in that direction, but it will be a few years before we have the answers."

In the meantime, panic over methane hydrates is probably premature. "There is a tendency in some quarters to latch on to a catastrophism scenario," she says. "That may sell newspapers, but it may not be the most responsible way to portray the science."

If you're the publisher of a sensationalist newspaper, take heart. There's still a good deal to fear when it comes to climate change. "I think the trajectory we're on with CO_2 [carbon dioxide] is very likely to lead to droughts that would be destabilizing to civilization. Another thing I worry about is sea-level rise," Archer says. "I think we have plenty to worry about with CO_2. We don't need methane hydrates in order to be very reasonably frightened about the future of our climate."

15

Climate Change Adaption and Disaster Risk Protection Will Be Challenges

Oxfam International

Oxfam International consists of thirteen organizations working worldwide to find lasting solutions to poverty and injustice.

Natural disasters are increasing as temperatures climb and rainfall intensifies. A rise in small- and medium-scale disasters has been recorded, yet extreme weather doesn't have to lead to catastrophe; it is poverty that renders people vulnerable. More and better emergency aid is needed, and humanitarian response must do more than save lives. It should bring about climate change adaptation and protect poor people's lives through a social safety net and disaster risk reduction.

The total number of natural disasters worldwide now averages 400–500 a year, up from an average of 125 in the early 1980s. The number of climate-related disasters, particularly floods and storms, is rising far faster than the number of geological disasters, such as earthquakes. Between 1980 and 2006, the number of floods and cyclones quadrupled from 60 to 240 a year while the number of earthquakes remained approximately the same, at around 20 a year. In 2007 the Oxfam International family of [non-governmental] agencies responded to floods or storms in more than 30 countries.

Disasters continue to happen in what the UN [United Nations] terms 'hotspots' of intensive risk, like Bangladesh, where

Oxfam International, "Climate Alarm: Disasters Increase as Climate Change Bites," Oxfam Briefing Paper, November 25, 2007. Reproduced by permission.

regularly occurring hazards—such as floods, storms, and cyclones—combine with growing numbers of people living in vulnerable conditions.

Countless lives have been saved through the provision of clean water, sanitation, shelter, food, and medical care.

There has been some improvement in dealing with big disasters in such hotspots—in preparing for them and, especially, in tackling the public health crises that can often follow major shocks. Countless lives have been saved through the provision of clean water, sanitation, shelter, food, and medical care to large numbers of people.

At the same time as climate hazards are growing in number, more people are being exposed to them because of poverty, powerlessness, population growth, and the movement and displacement of people to marginal areas. Over the past two decades, the number of people affected by disasters has increased from an average of 174 to 254 million people a year.

As a result of all these trends, small- and medium-scale disasters are occurring more frequently than the kind of large-scale disasters that hit the headlines. When a large number of localised disasters occur simultaneously, or follow one another very rapidly, as in West Africa, they can merge to become the kind of 'mega disaster' that Sir John Holmes [United Nations Under-Secretary-General for Humanitarian Affairs and Emergency Relief Coordinator] warned about.

According to Maarten van Aalst of the Red Cross/Red Crescent Climate Centre in the Netherlands, climate change is behind both more *unique events* and more *multiple* events. Unique events are those—such as storms, floods, or heatwaves—that are highly unusual in a region. 'These are of great concern as governments and communities are typically unprepared for them and only have a limited capacity to handle them', says van Aalst. Multiple events refer to situations where one area is affected by a series of, often different, disasters in a relatively short period of time. Both types of experience strain the coping capacities of governments and communities.

Heatwaves and Intense Rainfall

Two types of hazard are particularly noticeable. First, heat waves. In line with climate observations and predictions, the incidence of heatwaves has increased more than five-fold over the past 20 years, from 29 in 1987–1996 to 76 in 1997–2006. In Tajikistan, for instance, one of the world's most disaster-prone countries, agronomist Mirzokhonova Munavara told Oxfam workers:

> There has been a change in climate in the last 15 years. It gets extremely hot and then extremely cold. People are struggling because we have to adapt and we do not have the rain at times to water our land. The soil has become dry and crops have changed in quality and in colour. We have irrigation channels but no water. We cannot leave this village as we have nowhere to go and no money to leave. God has given us this weather so we will need to learn how to adapt, change our seeds so that we can continue to work and grow food.

The second is a trend towards more concentrated and more intense rainfall, causing or exacerbating flooding in countries as far apart as the UK [United Kingdom], Viet Nam, South Africa, Mexico, and India. For example, Manish Kumar Agrawal, Oxfam Programme Officer in Ahmedabad [India], reported:

> For the last three years, one trend which is coming up very clearly is that of very heavy rain in a very short duration (e.g. 500–600mm in just 24 hours). The number of such places affected is also increasing. For example, this year five districts of North Gujarat, which are considered as drought-prone, received very heavy rainfall (ranging from 200–

550mm in just 24 hours). The same phenomenon is happening in drought-prone Rajasthan.

Those societies that are being hardest hit by climate change, and which are likely to suffer most in the immediate future, are those that are least responsible for man-made greenhouse gas emissions.

Climatic disasters are on the increase as the Earth warms up—in line with scientific observations and computer simulations that model future climate.

Climatic disasters are on the increase as the Earth warms up—in line with scientific observations and computer simulations that model future climate. Scientists warn that an average global temperature rise of two degrees Celsius (3.6 degrees Fahrenheit) would be the threshold beyond which even more dangerous climate changes will become much more probable. Currently, temperatures are on track to go considerably higher than this. Such increases are likely to wreck the agricultural viability of whole regions of the world and destroy the livelihoods of millions of people, with appalling humanitarian consequences. In particular, 'hundreds of millions' more people will be exposed to increased water stress.

Poverty Makes People Vulnerable

The impact of a natural disaster is anything but natural: it is based on inequalities. In general, extreme climatic events in the rich world result in large economic losses and few deaths. In the poor world the impact is the other way round—greater loss of life and relatively less economic damage, because poor countries have fewer assets. But the damage can be proportionately more crippling. Between 1985 and 1999 the losses of the richest countries due to natural disasters were just over two per cent of GDP [gross domestic product], while the poorest countries' losses were 13 per cent.

Poverty increases the 'death to disaster' ratio. According to the International Federation of Red Cross [IFRC] and Red Crescent Societies, between 1991 and 2000 in the richest countries there were 23 deaths per disaster, compared with 1,052 deaths per disaster in the poorest countries. According to one analysis, 'in other words, development is an investment in disaster mitigation'.

The absolute numbers of people killed in disasters have been rising since the mid-1980s, but falling slightly as a proportion of overall population.

However, when mega-disasters such as the Asian tsunami of 2004 are discounted, the data show that average deaths per year from small and medium-scale climatic disasters more than doubled from nearly 6,000 in 1980 to over 14,000 in 2006, outpacing population growth. According to UN disaster risk reduction (DRR) experts: 'The rapid growth in the number of small-scale climatic disasters and of mortality in these events tends to indicate that extensive risk is increasing rapidly.'

The figures suggest that while investments in disaster preparedness have reduced vulnerability to mega disasters, they have failed to keep up with the rising frequency and severity of small ones.

Both floods and failures in rains, in particular, can dramatically accelerate the spread of debilitating and potentially deadly diseases such as diarrhoea.

Disproportionately Negative Effects

Vulnerability is a reflection of poverty and powerlessness—for example, having to live in a shack on a steep hillside in an urban slum, in danger from landslides. For poor people a succession of even relatively 'small' shocks—a week's delay in the rains, sickness in the family, getting into debt as a result—can be more damaging to livelihoods than the occasional big one. In the absence of any form of social safety net or insurance, people struggle to recover before the next shock hits, and this can lead to a spiral of destitution and greater vulnerability. Even relatively small changes in climate can have dire consequences. Both floods and failures in rains, in particular, can dramatically accelerate the spread of debilitating and potentially deadly diseases such as diarrhoea.

In an interview in Tajikistan, woman farmer Umeda Ddinaeva told Oxfam:

> Locusts attacked our fields and our entire crop has disappeared. I have noticed that when the temperature is above 34 degrees, when it is much hotter than usual, there is more chance that locusts will come. I will have to take out a loan to buy more seeds and spend the next two weeks getting the land ready to plant. It's expensive and we won't have an income for two months while the watermelons grow.

Globally, women depend most directly on natural resources to provide for their families: they are the main collectors of water and most women farmers depend on rain-fed agriculture, while at the same time women rarely own land and have minimum access to credit. They have fewer assets to fall back on than men have. Social constraints on women's involvement in public life may mean that they are the last and least to be informed and prepared for disasters, and the least able to access emergency aid after disasters. Drought and heatwaves, intense rain and floods and increasingly unpredictable seasons due to climate change are therefore likely to have disproportionately negative effects on women, potentially increasing their poverty and unequal status.

Prevention Is Better than Cure

The risk that a poor individual or household faces can be understood as a simple formula: risk = hazard x vulnerability. Protecting people's livelihoods and DRR can reduce risk.

Cuba provides an excellent case study of exemplary disaster preparedness built on pro-poor development policies. Typically, the number of people killed by hurricanes there every year is in single figures. A report by Oxfam America says: 'At the national level, Cuba's disaster legislation, public education on disasters, meteorological research, early warning system, effective communication system for emergencies, comprehensive emergency plan, and Civil Defence structure are important resources in avoiding disaster.

'At the local level, high levels of literacy, developed infrastructure in rural areas, and access to reliable health care are crucial for national efforts in disaster mitigation, preparation, and response.'

Knowing what the future climate is likely to bring allows governments and other actors to begin planning ahead and to undertake climate adaptation measures now.

Such examples are still, sadly, relatively uncommon, but Cuba is not completely alone. Bangladesh has made great strides in reducing the impact of the hazards that constantly assail it. In 1971 over 138,000 people perished in a cyclone. Subsequent cyclones—even the devastating cyclone that hit on 15 November [2007], the biggest since 1991—have killed far fewer people, due to the existence of cyclone shelters and greater community-based preparedness including evacuation plans, early warnings and the mobilisation of volunteers. In the Bangladesh countryside, 'raised villages' and flood shelters—artificial mounds the size of soccer pitches to which whole communities can retreat from floods—are fairly common sights. Mozambique too has got steadily better at implementing flood contingency plans, including providing essential services for displaced people (reducing recourse to international assistance).

Reducing vulnerability requires political will, particularly to put the most vulnerable people first—because they are usually the people with the least voice and influence in political decision-making. In East Africa, for instance, current climate models agree on the probability that much of that region will experience more intense rains. More rain could improve pasturelands, but a greening of semi-arid areas may also lure farmers to enclose pasture, pushing off pastoralists and their herds of animals and making them poorer and more vulnerable.

Knowing what the future climate is likely to bring allows governments and other actors to begin planning ahead and to undertake climate adaptation measures now. Viet Nam, for example, has effective systems for managing floods, but is less prepared for drought; the government could set up Drought Management Boards on the lines of its existing Flood Management Boards to tackle the new threat. Conversely, West African countries have drought and food shortage early warning systems (at national and regional levels), but are less ready to deal with floods. More intense rainfall will also increase soil erosion, which makes long-term soil conservation and water-harvesting measures even more necessary.

Humanitarian Funding Will Not Be Adequate

National governments are ultimately responsible for the welfare of their citizens, before, during, and after a disaster, and they should be best placed to respond in the most appropriate manner. It is when the disaster—whether a natural disaster or one due to conflict—is so great that it overwhelms their capacity to respond that timely, effective, and equitable international aid is needed.

Global humanitarian funding trends have been improving. A recent review concluded that there exists an increasing commitment to deliver timely and predictable funds that are both effective and equitable, a better appreciation of the links between relief and development, and a wider shared application of key principles.

However, there are still serious problems. Only around two-thirds of UN humanitarian appeals are met each year—and only one-third in the least-funded emergencies. For all emergencies, including war and conflict as well as natural disasters, the shortfall in humanitarian aid in 2006 was some US$1.7bn [billion]. The disbursement of aid is also still often skewed and is not based on humanitarian need. Visibility is a key factor; as the IFRC notes, 'there are even wider disparities between high profile, well-funded emergencies and those where people are relatively neglected.' Drought in a country like Niger might see funding per head of US$20. In a high profile crisis such as the South Asia earthquake funding per head can reach more than US$300.

The disbursement of aid is also still often skewed and is not based on humanitarian need.

If the rising trend in climatic disasters continues, can the system continue to cope? Both national governments and the international community have, to varying degrees, concentrated on, and have systems to respond to, large events, but are less prepared for small- to medium-scale crises. This points to the need to strengthen the capacities of local government and local communities and institutions, which should be better able to respond to these.

Climate Change and the Global Humanitarian System

It is firstly essential that action be taken to drastically reduce greenhouse gas emissions to bring global temperature increases swiftly under control and to keep global average temperature rise as far below two degrees Celsius as possible. Rich countries must act first and fastest to reduce emissions, and both rich and poor countries must start working together to find low-carbon pathways for future human development. The next UN climate change conference in Bali in December [2007] is a vital opportunity. If mitigation does not succeed, there is the very real prospect that growing climate-related disasters will overwhelm the humanitarian system and undermine development.

Regardless of emissions reductions, temperatures will continue to rise to some degree. Separate to funding for emergencies that will arise, Oxfam has estimated that developing countries will require at least US$50bn annually to adapt to unavoidable climate change. These funds should be provided by rich nations, in line with their responsibility for causing climate change and their capability to assist. Additional finance for adaptation is not aid, but a form of compensatory finance; it must not come out of long-standing donor commitments to provide 0.7 per cent of GDP as aid in order to eradicate poverty. At present, funding for adaptation is totally inadequate, and the Bali conference must mandate the search for new funds. Innovative financing mechanisms need to be explored. At the same time, commitment and political will is required in developing countries.

Humanitarian response must be timely and efficient and allocation must be . . . according to need.

The global volume of humanitarian funding remains inadequate and will need to increase. Major donor governments must keep the promises they made at the Gleneagles G8 Summit [major governments forum] to increase overseas development aid (ODA) by an additional US$50bn a year by 2010. This is a first requirement. If they do this, then humanitarian funding, which has persistently formed between seven per cent and ten per cent of total ODA, is likely to increase from

US$8.4bn in 2005 to over US$11bn. But it is currently a big "if"—two years on, aid to poor countries is falling, not rising. And that is without the challenge of climate change, which will require more. And although needs will vary from year to year, the aid has to be predictable and available when needed. Innovative financing mechanisms should also be explored.

Humanitarian response must be timely and efficient and allocation must be fair—i.e. according to need. It must be provided more swiftly in the crucial hours and days after disaster strikes, including through the improvement and expansion of pooled funding mechanisms like the UN's Central Emergency Response Fund (CERF), and by minimising the number of 'links in the chain' between the source of aid and beneficiaries on the ground. It must be appropriate—for example, shifting away from over-reliance on in-kind food aid towards more flexible solutions such as cash transfers.

Climate change is accentuating the fact that for many poor people, shocks are the norm. As well as more money for humanitarian response, more rounded approaches are needed to tackle human vulnerability. Governments must put poor people first and provide essential services like education and health. Aid should be used to build and protect the livelihoods and assets of poor people and should be provided over sustained periods, not just as 'humanitarian aid' in response to events when they occur. Long-term social protection systems— providing a regular income—and forms of insurance cushion people against shocks and can form the foundation for timely emergency scale-up when required. Governments are running social protection schemes of various kinds in several countries, and insurance schemes are being piloted in others—for example, against rain or crop failure.

Investing in Disaster Risk Reduction

Sustained investment in DRR and in climate-change adaptation saves lives and limits losses. In any disaster, it is the communities affected who are always first to respond, before governments or outside agencies can get there to help. Building up community capacity to prepare for and respond to disasters is crucial. In implementing DRR, governments and donors need to join up work on DRR both with planning for adaptation to climate change and with poverty reduction strategies. More work needs to be done to understand these linkages. Governments have made commitments to make their citizens safer from natural hazards through DRR; they need to put their promises into action by setting measurable targets, funding DRR adequately, and by building it into their plans and activities at all levels.

Humanitarian aid in crises should not only save lives, it should also seek to reduce the future vulnerability of populations at risk. This includes building the capacity of local actors, including government at all levels, and not displacing or undermining them; and empowering affected populations so that they are not simply recipients of assistance, but have a strong voice in response and in subsequent recovery and rehabilitation measures. There is an important need to invest in better meteorological data-gathering systems and early-warning communication systems, especially radio, and to raise public awareness of climate change.

Just as provision of essential services like health, education, water and sanitation build the resilience of communities and reduce risk, so inappropriate and unsustainable development strategies not only waste scant resources, they also end up putting more people at risk. Oxfam has recently expressed such fears about the current "dash for biofuels". Failure to tackle poverty, especially rural poverty, is one reason for increased rates of deforestation in many countries, increasing greenhouse gas emissions and raising the risk of mudslides and flooding. Development aid should integrate analyses of disaster risk and climate trends.

Organizations to Contact

The editors have compiled the following list of organizations concerned with the issues debated in this book. The descriptions are derived from materials provided by the organizations. All have publications or information available for interested readers. The list was compiled on the date of publication of the present volume; the information provided here may change. Be aware that many organizations take several weeks or longer to respond to inquiries, so allow as much time as possible.

Aon Benfield UCL Hazard Research Centre
Department of Earth Sciences, University College London
136 Gower St. (Lewis Building), London   WC1E 6BT
  UK
+44 (0)20 7679 3637 • fax: +44 (0)20 7679 2390
e-mail: info@abuhrc.org
Web site: www.abuhrc.org

The Aon Benfield UCL Hazard Research Centre facilitates the improvement of natural hazard and risk assessment and the reduction of exposure to natural catastrophes. The Aon Benfield Centre publishes the *Alert* newsletter, an annual *Hazard and Risk Science Review*, as well as articles and books, which are available to view online.

**Disaster Research Center at the University
of Delaware (DRC)**
166 Graham Hall, Newark, DE   19716
(302) 831-6618 • fax: (302) 831-2091
Web site: www.udel.edu/DRC/

The Disaster Research Center conducts field and survey research on group, organizational and community preparation for, response to, and recovery from natural and technological disasters and other community-wide crises. DRC researchers have carried out systematic studies on a broad range of disaster types, including hurricanes, floods, earthquakes, tornadoes, hazardous chemical incidents, and plane crashes. The DRC Web site provides links to research institutions and information on its own findings.

Earthquake Engineering Research Institute (EERI)
499 14th St., Suite 320, Oakland, CA   94612-1934
(510) 451-0905 • fax: (510) 451-5411
Web site: www.eeri.org/

The Earthquake Engineering Research Institute is a national, nonprofit, technical society of engineers, geoscientists, architects, planners, public officials, and social scientists. The objective of EERI is to reduce earthquake risk by advancing the science and practice of earthquake engineering, and by improving understanding of the impact of earthquakes on the physical, social, economic, political, and cultural environment. It also advocates comprehensive and realistic measures for reducing the harmful effects of earthquakes. The institute publishes a newsletter.

Natural Hazards Center
University of Colorado at Boulder, 482 UCB
Boulder, CO   80309-0482
(303) 492-6818 • fax: (303) 492-2151
e-mail: hazctr@colorado.edu
Web site: www.colorado.edu/hazards

The Natural Hazards Center is a national and international clearinghouse of knowledge concerning the social science and policy aspects of disasters. The center collects and shares research and experience related to preparedness for, response to, and recovery from disasters. It publishes the bimonthly newsletter, the *Natural Hazards Observer*, and the electronic biweekly newsletter, *Disaster Research*. In addition, the center maintains a Web site of updated information on upcoming conferences and links to publications, organizations, and other Internet resources for hazards research and practice.

Prepare.org
Web site: www.prepare.org/

This Web site is maintained by the American Red Cross and other community-based organizations to help families prepare for natural and human-caused disasters. Preparedness materials are available in English and multiple foreign languages. The site also offers a free online preparedness training module.

United Nations International Strategy for Disaster Reduction (UNISDR)
Palais des Nations, Geneva 10   CH-1211
    Switzerland
+41 22 917 8908/8907 • fax: +41 22 917 8964
e-mail: isdr@un.org
Web site: www.unisdr.org

The UNISDR aims to build disaster-resilient communities. Its goal is the reduction of human, social, economic and environmental losses due to natural hazards and related technological and environmental disasters. The UNISDR maintains a library on disaster reduction and selected bibliographies, and also a Web site for the promotion of early warning.

U.S. Centers for Disease Control (CDC) – Emergency Preparedness and Response
Centers for Disease Control and Prevention, 1600 Clifton Rd.
Atlanta, GA   30333
(800) CDC-INFO (800-232-4636)
e-mail: cdcinfo@cdc.gov
Web site: www.bt.cdc.gov/disasters/

Preparing people for emerging health threats is one of the CDC's main goals. The CDC contributes to national, state, and local efforts to prepare for and prevent public health disasters before they occur. When a disaster has occurred, the CDC is prepared to respond and support national, state, and local partners in responding in order to improve public health outcomes. After response to a disaster has ended, the CDC assists national, state, and local partners in the recovery and restoration of public health functions. A number of resources are available on its Web site.

U.S. Federal Emergency Management Agency (FEMA)
500 C St. SW, Washington, DC   20472
(800) 621-FEMA (3362)
Web site: www.fema.gov

The Federal Emergency Management Agency is part of the U.S. Department of Homeland Security (DHS). The primary mission of FEMA is to reduce the loss of life and property and protect the nation from all hazards, including natural disasters, acts of terrorism, and other man-made disasters. FEMA offers a variety of disaster information on its Web site.

United States Geological Survey (USGS) Earthquake Hazards Program
USGS National Center, 12201 Sunrise Valley Dr.
Reston, VA   20192
(703) 648-4000
Web site: http://earthquake.usgs.gov/

The USGS provides scientific information to describe and understand the Earth; minimize loss of life and property from natural disasters; manage water, biological, energy, and mineral resources; and enhance and protect the quality of life. The USGS maintains the Earth Science Library and provides podcasts on its Web site.

Bibliography

Books

Patrick Abbott   *Natural Disasters*. Boston:
                    McGraw-Hill Higher Education,
                    2004.

Cynthia Ball, ed.   *Help! A Survivor's Guide to Emergency
                    Preparedness*. Alberta, Canada:
                    Museums Alberta, 2003.

Kristin Bates and   *Through the Eye of Katrina: Social
Richelle Swan,   Justice in the United States*. Durham,
eds.   NC: Carolina Academic Press, 2007.

Walter Brasch   *'Unacceptable': The Federal
                    Government's Response to Hurricane
                    Katrina*. Charleston, SC: BookSurge,
                    2006.

Douglas Brinkley   *The Great Deluge: Hurricane Katrina,
                    New Orleans, and the Mississippi Gulf
                    Coast*. New York: William Morrow,
                    2006.

Edward Bryant   *Tsunami: the Underrated Hazard*.
                    New York: Cambridge University
                    Press, 2001.

John Brown   *Hurricane Katrina: Response and
Childs, ed.   Responsibilities*. Santa Cruz, CA: New
                    Pacific Press, 2007.

Damon Coppola   *Introduction to International Disaster
                    Management*. Boston: Butterworth
                    Heinemann, 2007.

Ronald Daniels, *On Risk and Disaster: Lessons from*
Donald F. Kettl, *Hurricane Katrina*. Philadelphia:
and Howard University of Pennsylvania Press,
Kunreuther, eds. 2006.

Jennifer Housley *Treating Victims of Mass Disaster and Terrorism*. Cambridge, MA: Hogrefe & Huber Publishers, 2007.

Robert Kovach *Firefly Guide to Global Hazards*. Buffalo, NY: Firefly Books, 2004.

John McQuaid *Path of Destruction: The Devastation*
and Mark *of New Orleans and the Coming Age*
Schleifstein *of Superstorms*. New York: Little, Brown, and Company, 2006.

National Center *Emergency Giving: The Role of Family*
for Family *Donors in Relief, Recovery, and*
Philanthropy *Rebuilding*. Washington, DC: The National Center for Family Philanthropy, 2005.

Natural *Learning from Catastrophe: Quick*
Hazards Center *Response Research in the Wake of Hurricane Katrina*. Boulder, CO: Institute of Behavioral Science, University of Colorado at Boulder, 2006.

Thomas Neff *Holding Out and Hanging On: Surviving Hurricane Katrina*. Columbia, MO: University of Missouri Press, 2007.

A.G. Robinson   *Earthshock: Hurricanes, Volcanoes, Earthquakes, Tornadoes, and Other Forces of Nature.* New York: Thames & Hudson, 2002.

Keith Smith   *Environmental Hazards: Assessing Risk and Reducing Disaster.* New York: Routledge, 2002.

Nicolas Wade, ed.   *The Science Times Book of Natural Disasters.* New York: Lyons Press, 2000.

Periodicals

Barbara Allen   "Environmental Justice and Expert Knowledge in the Wake of a Disaster," *Social Studies of Science,* vol. 37, no. 1, 2007.

Jonathan Shapiro Anjaria   "Urban Calamities: A View from Mumbai," *Space and Culture,* vol. 9, no. 1, 2006.

Diane Austin   "Coastal Exploitation, Land Loss, and Hurricanes: A Recipe for Disaster," *American Anthropologist,* vol. 108, no. 4, 2006.

Kulwinder Banipal   "Strategic Approach to Disaster Management: Lessons Learned from Hurricane Katrina," *Disaster Prevention and Management,* vol. 15, no. 3, 2006.

Yudhijit Bhattacharjee   "In Wake of Disaster, Scientists Seek out Clues to Prevention," *Science,* January 2005.

Celeste Biever   "How to Predict an Eruption," *New Scientist*, December 2004.

Jessica Binns   "Ground Monitoring System May Prevent Massive Losses in Natural Disaster," *Civil Engineering*, September 2004.

William Broad   "Deadly and yet Necessary, Quakes Renew the Planet," *New York Times*, January 2005.

David Brooks   "Katrina's Silver Lining," *New York Times*, September 8, 2005.

David Cyranoski   "Deluge of Typhoons May Aid Forecast Models," *Nature*, October 2004.

Norman A.   "Hurricane Disaster Response by
Dolch, Daniel L.   School-Based Health Centers,"
Meyer, and Angel   *Children, Youth and Environments*,
V. Huval   2008.

FEMA, Heritage   "Before and After Disasters; Federal
Preservation,   Funding for Cultural Institutions,"
and National   *FEMA 533*, September 2005.
Endowment for
the Arts

Donna Gaffney   "The Aftermath of Disaster: Children in Crisis," *Journal of Clinical Psychology*, 2006.

Andrew Garrett, Roy Grant, Paula Madrid, Arturo Brito, David Abramson, and Irwin Redlener — "Children and Megadisasters: Lessons Learned in the New Millennium," *Advances in Pediatrics*, 2007.

John Harrald — "Agility and Discipline: Critical Success Factors for Disaster Response," *The Annals of the American Academy of Political and Social Science*, March 2006.

Thomas Hayden — "Preventing Disaster," *U.S. News & World Report*, January 2005.

Christopher Henke — "Situation Normal? Repairing a Risky Ecology," *Social Studies of Science*, 2007.

Donald Kettl — "Is the Worst Yet to Come?" *Annals of the American Academy of Political and Social Science*, 2006.

Eli Kintisch — "U.S. Clamor Grows for Global Network of Ocean Sensors," *Science*, January 2005.

Anne Westbrook Lauten and Kimberly Lietz — "A Look at the Standards Gap: Comparing Child Protection Responses in the Aftermath of Hurricane Katrina and the Indian Ocean Tsunami," *Children, Youth and Environments*, 2008.

Madeleine Nash — "What's Behind California's Wild Weather?" *Time*, January 2005.

New York Times   "Urgent Warning Proved Prescient,"
                          September 7, 2005.

Rena Pacella   "Need Another Reason to Lose Sleep?
                          Scientists Say We're Ill-Prepared for
                          Devastating Tsunamis," *Popular
                          Science*, November 2004.

Charles Perrow   "Using Organizations: The Case of
                          FEMA," *Homeland Security Affairs*,
                          2005.

John Schwartz   "Text Messaging Pushed for Use as
                          Disaster Warning Systems," *New York
                          Times*, December 2004.

Michael Taverna   "Early Warning," *Aviation Week &
                          Space Technology*, January 2005.

Simon Winchester   "The Year the Earth Fought Back,"
                          New York Times, December 2004.

Index